THE GOOD, THE BAD, AND THE UGLY
SEATTLE SEAHAWKS

HEART-POUNDING, JAW-DROPPING, AND GUT-WRENCHING MOMENTS FROM SEATTLE SEAHAWKS HISTORY

Chris Cluff

TRIUMPH
BOOKS

Copyright © 2007 by Chris Cluff

No part of this publication may be reproduced, stored in a retrieval system, or transmitted in any form by any means, electronic, mechanical, photocopying, or otherwise, without the prior written permission of the publisher, Triumph Books, 542 South Dearborn Street, Suite 750, Chicago, Illinois 60605.

Triumph Books and colophon are registered trademarks of Random House, Inc.

Library of Congress Cataloging-in-Publication Data

Cluff, Chris, 1970–
    The good, the bad, and the ugly Seattle Seahawks / by Chris Cluff.
        p. cm.
    Includes bibliographical references.
    ISBN-13: 978-1-57243-977-1
    ISBN-10: 1-57243-977-7
    1. Seattle Seahawks (Football team). I. Title. II. Title: Seattle Seahawks.

GV956.S4C48 2007
796.332'6409797772—dc22

2007014873

This book is available in quantity at special discounts for your group or organization. For further information, contact:

Triumph Books
542 South Dearborn Street
Suite 750
Chicago, Illinois 60605
(312) 939-3330
Fax (312) 663-3557

Printed in U.S.A.
ISBN: 978-1-57243-977-1
Design by Patricia Frey
All photos courtesy of AP/Wide World Photos, except where otherwise indicated.

This book is dedicated to my dad, Bruce, who instilled in me a love for football and turned me into a Seahawks fan back in their early days. Thanks, Dad.

CONTENTS

FOREWORD

Chris Cluff has authored a very interesting and entertaining look at the Seahawks franchise and its history. I was mesmerized as I read stories I had long forgotten. Chris has done an excellent job of retelling the stories in an interesting and accurate manner. I found myself laughing and crying as he told many stories that I actually had a part in.

Anyone interested in the history of the Seahawks or, more generally, in the NFL, will love this story. It is the story of uncommon faith and loyalty of Seahawks fans and supporters; players—good, bad, and otherwise; loyal coaches; and a vacillating ownership that has changed hands on two different occasions.

At the end of the day, this is a story about the Northwest and its unbelievable can-do spirit. And its team—the Seattle Seahawks! The good, the bad, and the ugly! While the team has certainly seen a fluctuating win-loss record, questionable college drafts, strange coaching decisions, etc., the one constant has been the incredibly loyal and faithful Seahawks fans! And this book is for you!

—Steve Largent

INTRODUCTION

When the Seahawks finally made their way to their first Super Bowl at the end of the 2005 season, it was the culmination of a 30-year quest to reach the NFL's championship game. They didn't win the title, but they accomplished more than any squad in club history.

A young franchise by NFL standards, the Seahawks nonetheless had gone through a lot on their way to their first Super Bowl—from the up-and-down early years under Jack Patera to the perennial playoff teams of Chuck Knox to the barren Behring years. They had endured two player strikes in the 1980s, Curt Warner's knee injury, Kenny Easley's forced retirement, Brian Bosworth's bombastic arrival, three first-round flakes at quarterback, a nightmarish 1992 season, a madcap move to Los Angeles, and a power struggle between their president and their coach. But they had gone to the playoffs with guys like Easley, Warner, Steve Largent, Dave Krieg, Jacob Green, and Joe Nash; they had put together a great defense in the early 1990s; and they finally had become a constant contender under Mike Holmgren in the 2000s.

The 2005 Seahawks realized what their success meant to the old generation, which had for 20 years carried the torch as the best group of Seahawks ever.

As the 2005 team prepared to play the Washington Redskins in search of the Seahawks' first playoff win since 1984, quarterback Matt Hasselbeck said, "The thing I've learned through the course of this week is that it means a lot to a lot of people. Some of those people are former players here. Some of those people are coaches that have been around or people in the [team headquarters] building. Or maybe it's just some of the people from Seattle that have followed the team since 1976. It would mean a great deal to them. For that reason, to see the kind of support that those people have given our team makes it a little more special if, in fact, we are able to get it done."

With the old Seahawks watching, the next generation indeed got it done against Washington and then beat the Carolina Panthers to reach the Super Bowl for the first time.

With that success, Triumph Books decided it was the perfect time to recount the highs and lows—the people, plays, games, and events—that shaped the Seattle Seahawks through their first 30 years. So here it is—a compilation of the best and worst stories in franchise history: the good, bad, and ugly of Seahawks football.

THE GOOD

FORT KNOX

When Curt Warner took off down the right sideline for a 60-yard gain against Kansas City on his first NFL carry in 1983, it was obvious the Seahawks had changed. They had become Ground Chuck, a team that under new coach Chuck Knox planned to rely on its stud running back and a tougher defense.

While the defense didn't come around as quickly as Knox hoped it would, giving up the most yards in franchise history, Warner more than lived up to his status as the number three pick in the 1983 draft and helped the Seahawks reach the playoffs for the first time and establish themselves as perennial playoff contenders for the rest of the decade.

Warner gave the Seahawks the game-breaking running back they had not had throughout their first seven seasons. In his first season he set team records with 335 carries, 1,449 yards, six 100-yard games, and the first 200-yard rushing performance in team history. He also led the AFC with 14 touchdowns. It all earned him a Pro Bowl berth and awards for AFC rookie of the year and offensive player of the year.

Quarterback Dave Krieg had seen it coming in training camp when he handed the ball to Warner and saw how he cut to daylight, making something out of nothing. "He made a couple moves and got through the hole so fast. He was quick in the hole. His will to get yards was incredible."

While Warner was the biggest acquisition in 1983, Knox made a few other key moves that paid off. He brought in veteran linemen Blair Bush and Reggie McKenzie and tight end Charle Young. But even with those additions, the Seahawks didn't look all that different from the 1982 team, which had gone 4–5 in a strike-shortened season during which coach Jack Patera had been fired.

With his team scuffling along at 4–3 and trailing the Pittsburgh Steelers 24–0 at halftime at the Kingdome, Knox decided he needed to make one more change. He replaced quarterback Jim Zorn, who had started 100 games since the team was created in 1976, with Krieg, the former undrafted free agent who would soon

Former Seahawks head coach Chuck Knox looks at a portrait of himself during his induction into the Seahawks Ring of Honor in 2005. He coached the Seahawks from 1983 to 1991.

be known far and wide as the guy from "now-defunct" Milton College. Krieg nearly rallied the Seahawks against the Steelers— Seattle lost 27–21—and gave the offense some confidence.

Paul Moyer, a rookie safety in 1983 who has been with the club for nearly every season since as a player, coach, or broadcaster, calls the Pittsburgh game the turning point of that season.

"We lost, but obviously it was the beginning of Krieg's career as the starting quarterback," Moyer said. "We had a lot of confidence in Krieg, and he had a lot of confidence in himself. Dave had that 'just gonna let it fly' mentality."

In the first seven and a half games, Zorn had completed barely 50 percent of his passes, with seven touchdowns and seven interceptions. Krieg was stellar in his place, hitting 60.5 percent of his throws and tossing 18 touchdowns and 11 interceptions. Krieg's passer rating of 95.0 that season still stands as the best in team history.

"Dave was a guy that every time he got in the game, you couldn't figure out how he got the ball in the end zone. But he was able to do that," Hall of Fame receiver Steve Largent said. "We just sort of laughed about how he could move the ball. He threw sidearmed or ran around and scrambled to make a throw. But he kept the ball moving. He was a super-competitive guy and a lot more talented than people gave him credit for. But he never knew it."

Krieg sparked the Seahawks to wins in their next two games. They still were just 6–6, though, when they hosted the Kansas City Chiefs on November 27 in a game that gave them the confidence they needed. Warner rushed for a team-record 207 yards and scored three times, and Norm Johnson kicked the tying and winning field goals as the Seahawks won 51–48 in overtime, the highest-scoring game since the NFL and AFL merged in 1970.

"Going through the season, the team didn't know how to win yet. We were floundering around .500," Moyer said. "But in the Kansas City game, our team said, 'Whoa! Maybe the magic's on our side.'"

The Seahawks were blown out by the Dallas Cowboys the next week, but they got some more magic in the penultimate contest at the Meadowlands, where the Seahawks faced the

SEAHAWKS ALL-TIME TEAM

QB	Dave Krieg
RB	Shaun Alexander
FB	John L. Williams
WR	Steve Largent
WR	Brian Blades
TE	Mike Tice
OT	Walter Jones
OG	Steve Hutchinson
C	Robbie Tobeck
OG	Bryan Millard
OT	Howard Ballard
DE	Jacob Green
DT	Cortez Kennedy
DT	Joe Nash
DE	Michael Sinclair
LB	Chad Brown
LB	Fredd Young
LB	Keith Butler
CB	Dave Brown
CB	Shawn Springs
S	Kenny Easley
S	Eugene Robinson
K	Norm Johnson
P	Rick Tuten
KR	Steve Broussard
PR	Joey Galloway
ST	Rufus Porter

Giants, who were struggling in Bill Parcells's first season as coach.

Jacob Green had been complaining and waiting for it all day. Held by Giants right tackle John Tautolo all game, the star defensive end finally drew the flag on the most important play as the Seahawks held a tenuous 17–12 lead.

As Jeff Rutledge dropped back to throw a 10-yard touchdown pass to Earnest Gray with 25 seconds left, Tautolo put his best wrestling move on Green—and referee Jerry Markbreit finally flagged him for it. The touchdown was called back, and the Giants failed to convert fourth-and-17 when Kerry Justin and Keith Simpson broke up Rutledge's pass to Byron Williams at the 2-yard line.

"That was big," Moyer said. "If we lose that game, we don't make the playoffs. That was a big one."

In a winner-gets-in game in the season finale at the Kingdome, the Seahawks took care of the New England Patriots 24–6 to set up a rematch with the Denver Broncos.

The Seahawks had split the season series, winning 27–19 at the Kingdome and losing 38–27 in Denver. The Seahawks hosted the wild-card playoff game because they had won their final game while the Broncos had lost to Kansas City. With the home-field advantage of the Kingdome behind him, Krieg completed 12 of 13 passes and threw three touchdown passes as the Seahawks dominated 31–7 behind a defense that was gaining confidence despite having surrendered 6,029 yards that season (a number that stood as the most in franchise history until the 2000 team surrendered 6,391).

The Seahawks then went to Miami as huge underdogs and pulled off a 27–20 upset on a comeback led by Krieg, Warner, Largent, and Seattle's special teams (see chapter 6). That set up the Seahawks for a surprising trip to the AFC Championship Game, and that's where the dream ride came to a crashing halt in a 30–14 blowout at the hands of the Los Angeles Raiders.

"Here I am coming from Milton College and planning to go to the Super Bowl," Krieg said of his inexperience, which reflected the youth of the entire Seattle team. "That's where the Raiders had a big advantage. They had been there before, so they knew what it took. We were in way over our heads."

1984: NO WARNER, NO PROBLEM

After the amazing run to the AFC title game, the Seahawks entered 1984 with Super Bowl expectations for the first time in franchise history.

It looked like they were ready to live up to them when they pounded Cleveland 33–0 in the first game of the season—the first time the Seahawks had ever won their opening game. The high hopes came crashing down, however, when Warner suffered a torn anterior cruciate ligament in his knee while running a sweep play.

"When it happened, the place went dead silent. Really quiet," Moyer recalled of the Kingdome. "As a team, we could have lost it. He clearly was a special player. Morale was certainly low. But this is where Chuck Knox probably doesn't get credit for being as great a coach as he was. He was a big believer in 'the next guy steps up.' Injuries were not an excuse. He assured us that we were going to have a big season still. Defensively, we had to step it up more."

Said Largent: "We lost him [Warner] and basically had a ragtag backfield of running backs—Dan Doornink, Eric Lane, and a host of other guys. Everybody was disappointed, particularly Curt. But

I don't think any of us thought the season was over. We knew our whole season didn't ride on one running back."

Instead it rode on the shotgun arm of Krieg and a defense led by the guy who would become the NFL's defensive player of the year, safety Kenny Easley.

The defense, which had such a tough time in 1983, was much improved in 1984 because "everybody knew their role," Moyer said. Krieg and Moyer both credited defensive coordinator Tom Catlin with bringing the unit together.

"Kenny Easley, Dave Brown, and Jacob Green were the leaders," Moyer said. "We had a difficult front three with Green, Joe Nash, and Jeff Bryant. The secondary was incredibly smart. John Harris, Easley, and Dave Brown were extremely bright."

"It was a difficult defense to line up against," Moyer added. "People told us all the time, 'You guys do so much, it's hard to game plan against.'"

The result was one of the best units in franchise history. It set a team record for fewest points allowed (282), most sacks (55), and yards lost on sacks (398). Topped by Easley's 10 interceptions, the Seahawks led the league and set a team record with 38 picks. They returned a team-record seven of them for touchdowns. Easley, Brown (a career-high eight interceptions), and Nash (82 tackles and seven sacks) all were voted to the Pro Bowl.

The best defensive performances of the season came in back-to-back shutouts of San Diego and Kansas City at midseason. Easley intercepted three passes in a 24–0 win over the Chargers in San Diego, and the secondary intercepted a team-record six passes and set an NFL record by returning four of them for touchdowns in a 45–0 blowout of the Kansas City Chiefs at the Kingdome. Brown tied an NFL record by taking two back for scores.

The Chiefs threw the ball 55 times in that game—the most anyone had ever thrown against Seattle.

"We were pass rushing every single play," Nash recalled. "Jimmy Rourke, who was playing tackle for the Chiefs, says, 'Geez you aren't killing us bad enough?'... Nothing went right for them that day."

With Curt Warner lost to injury in 1984, the offensive burden fell onto the shoulders of quarterback Dave Krieg.

With all that help from the high-scoring defense, the Seahawks set a team scoring record (418 points) that wouldn't be broken until the 2005 Super Bowl Seahawks scored 452.

"The defense had so many turnovers," Krieg said. "They played spectacular. They owed it to Tom Catlin, who took a lot of guys and brought them together."

Even without Warner, the offense came together behind Krieg. The fifth-year veteran set team records with 3,671 passing yards and 32 touchdowns and joined Largent (74 catches, 1,164 yards, 12 touchdowns) in the Pro Bowl.

"Curt got hurt," Krieg said, "and so now we've got to throw the ball a lot more. We end up winning with the defense creating turnovers and throwing the ball. We turned into Air Chuck."

The Seahawks won eight straight games, a team record that lasted until the 2005 team won 11 straight.

From a 31–28 win over Buffalo on October 14 through a 38–17 blowout against Detroit on December 2, they didn't drop a game. They won 12 of their first 14 games.

"We were on such a roll, we didn't believe we'd lose," Moyer said.

But they did. In Kansas City Bill Kenney threw for 312 yards and two touchdowns, and the Chiefs intercepted six passes in a 34–7 retributive strike that made up for the 45–0 blanking they had suffered at the Kingdome a month before. Krieg, who had thrown for 700 yards and eight touchdowns the previous two weeks in wins against Denver and Detroit, threw five interceptions and just one touchdown pass against the Chiefs.

That loss set up a huge game in the season finale at the Kingdome against the Broncos, who were tied with the Seahawks at 12–3. The winner would win the AFC West.

The Seahawks intercepted four of John Elway's throws in the first half, but Denver used two turnovers early in the third quarter to take a 17-point lead in what became a 31–14 win. The Broncos gained the first-round bye and home game that came with the division title while the Seahawks had to play in the first round against the defending Super Bowl champion Los Angeles Raiders.

The Raiders had easily handled the Seahawks in the AFC Championship Game the previous season on the way to winning the Super Bowl. But the Seahawks were no longer intimidated. Doornink ran for 123 yards and Krieg hit Daryl Turner with a 26-yard touchdown pass as the Seahawks won 13–7 in what turned out to be the last playoff win for the Seattle franchise until the 2005 team won twice on its way to the Super Bowl.

The next week, the Seahawks traveled to Miami for the second straight year to play the Dolphins, who had gone 14–2 that season. Dan Marino, their second-year star, threw three touchdown passes as the Dolphins avenged the 1983 upset loss with a 31–10 win in what Miami receiver Mark Clayton called "get-back day."

The Seahawks had fallen short of the Super Bowl again, but they had overcome the loss of one of their best players and put together the best season in team history.

"We lost Curt Warner, and everybody played better," Krieg said. "Our defense played well, role players played well, we figured out how to win games. It was a fun, fun year."

THE BLUE ANGEL

Sure, Steve Largent ended up with every major NFL receiving record by the time he retired in 1989. But one of the most satisfying moments of his career had nothing to do with records. It was all about payback.

Amid all of Largent's records and honors and off-field works and his reputation as one of the classiest men in NFL history, Largent's hit on Denver safety Mike Harden still stands as one of the most memorable plays in Seattle sports history.

It was a fortuitous opportunity for Largent, who took full advantage of his chance to get revenge on Harden for a savage forearm hit in the 1988 season opener that mangled Largent's face mask, dislodged two teeth, and knocked the 34-year-old receiver unconscious and out of the game.

"I was out before I hit the ground," Largent recalled. "It was probably the hardest I'd ever been hit in my life. It's one of those plays you don't forget."

The Seahawks managed to win 21–14, but Largent had no chance to make Harden and the Broncos pay for the brutal hit that ended up costing Harden a $5,000 fine. That is, until the rematch three months later.

In a Sunday night game televised by ESPN, the Seahawks hosted the Broncos at the Kingdome, and Largent got his chance for payback. Early in the first half, Harden intercepted a pass from Dave Krieg in the end zone and ran toward the left sideline as he sought to elude the Seahawks' offensive players. From behind, Largent streaked toward Harden like a heat-seeking missile.

"I'm running after Harden, and he doesn't see me coming," Largent said. "He cut across the field, and I hit him with everything I had."

Krieg knew Largent was reveling in the retributive strike. "Steve stands over him like a heavyweight champ who had just knocked him out. Then he sees the ball rolling around and picks it up, remembering, 'That's right, there's a football game going on.'"

Steve Largent comes down with a catch in his record-tying 127th consecutive game, a streak he'd eventually run to 177 games.

The Seahawks went on to pound the Broncos 42–14, eliminating Denver from the playoffs and setting up Seattle for its first AFC West title the next week.

Said Largent: "People asked me later: 'Did you know it was Mike Harden?' I absolutely knew. And I hit him with everything I had. It was one of the most satisfying moments in my career."

It's also one of the most memorable plays in Seattle sports history because it came from one of the most mild-mannered and least intimidating players in NFL history. As a poster depicting Largent in a flight suit once called him, he was the "Blue Angel"— a soft-spoken, good-hearted, classy Christian man who just happened to be one of the best wide receivers in the league.

Largent retired in 1989 with six major NFL records. A seven-time Pro Bowl player, Largent was so revered in Seattle that he became the first member of the Seahawks' Ring of Honor when he was inducted before his final game. He was so respected in the NFL that he was inducted into the Pro Football Hall of Fame in 1995, his first year of eligibility. And, at that time, the Seahawks also retired his No. 80, which joined No. 12 (see chapter 8) as the only numbers to be retired by the franchise.

Not bad for a guy the Houston Oilers didn't want—even though they had drafted him in the fourth round of the 1976 draft. Seattle assistant Jerry Rhome had been on the coaching staff at Tulsa, where Largent played college ball, and Rhome recommended Largent to coach Jack Patera. So the Seahawks procured the receiver from Houston for a mere eighth-round pick just before Seattle's first season began.

Largent immediately played beyond the limits that seemed to be placed upon him by his size (5'11" and 191 pounds) and lack of great speed. He was a classic overachiever, getting by—no, dominating—with guile, great hand-eye coordination, and precise route-running.

"Steve Largent was very similar to [the late cornerback] Dave Brown, a consummate professional, always working on his technique," Krieg said. "He was very studious of the defense he was going against. He could read the secondary just running the route."

Safety Kenny Easley once said: "What separates Steve from the rest of the receivers is that he has a knack for running routes that others don't have. He manipulates defensive backs; he dissects them. He has a phenomenal ability to 'sight adjust' on a pass route, meaning when a defensive back isn't right where he is supposed to be, Steve will make a spur-of-the-moment adjustment in his route to get open."

Linebacker Dave Wyman compared Largent's innate ability to lose defenders on pass routes to the corkscrew moves of Barry Sanders: "I was always amazed at how he could get guys twisted the wrong way. I could not believe the space he could create, how open he could get."

Largent put that talent to work immediately, finishing third in the NFC with 54 receptions in 1976. In 1978 he led the AFC with 71 receptions, recorded his first of eight 1,000-yard seasons, and went to his first Pro Bowl. In 1979 he led the NFL with 1,237 receiving yards. And it went on like that for 14 seasons.

By the end of it, Largent held six major NFL receiving records—most receptions (819), most consecutive games with a catch (177), most receiving yards (13,089), most receiving touchdowns (100), most seasons with 50 or more receptions (10), and most seasons with 1,000 receiving yards (8).

He has since been passed in every statistical receiving category by players from the air-it-out generation of the 1990s and 2000s. But since he didn't expect to ever hold any of those records, it certainly does not bother him.

"I never thought I'd be breaking anybody's records for anything," he said. "But now my records have all been broken and eclipsed by several players. I still say my career was like a dream. The older I get, the less I can believe what I did."

A man of strong Christian faith, Largent believed in helping out off the field, too. When his son Kramer was born with spina bifida, Largent and his wife had a personal interest in trying to find a cure for that defect. They became big backers of the Spina Bifida Foundation, and Steve and Kramer appeared in an NFL-sponsored United Way commercial. In 1988 Largent was named the NFL's Man of the Year. And in 1989 the Seahawks made the receiver the first recipient of the Steve Largent Award, which players vote annually to give to the player who best exemplifies the spirit, dedication, and integrity of the Seahawks.

Largent tried to put his values to work in the U.S. House of Representatives in the 1990s, when he was a four-term congressman for his Oklahoma district. He left public office in 2002, when he barely lost the Oklahoma gubernatorial race.

KEY MOMENTS IN STEVE LARGENT'S CAREER

October 6, 1986: On the national stage of *Monday Night Football*, the Seahawks destroy San Diego 33–7 and Largent sets an NFL record by catching a pass in his 128th consecutive game.

December 27, 1987: Largent catches six passes in a 41–20 loss at Kansas City and becomes the NFL's all-time leading receiver with 751 catches, breaking Charlie Joiner's record of 750.

September 18, 1988: In a 17–6 loss in San Diego, Largent sets the NFL record for receiving yards (12,167), breaking Charlie Joiner's old mark (12,146).

December 11, 1988: In one of the most apropos payback moments in sports history, Largent blasts Denver safety Mike Harden during an interception return and forces a fumble by the safety who had knocked the receiver out of the season opener with a dirty hit. Largent and the Seahawks add insult to injury by blowing out Denver, 42–14.

December 10, 1989: Largent records the NFL-record 100th touchdown of his career in Seattle's 24–17 win in Cincinnati. It was vintage Largent, as he went high in the back of the end zone and tapped both feet in bounds before falling out.

December 23, 1989: Before an unbefitting 29–0 loss to Washington, Largent is fêted in a pregame ceremony in which the Seahawks make him the first man inducted into the team's Ring of Honor.

It all made him one of the most respected sports figures of his generation and certainly one of the most revered athletes to ever play in Seattle.

When Largent retired in 1989, former NFL commissioner Pete Rozelle told reporters, "It took only seven months to find my successor [Paul Tagliabue], but it will be years before anyone with the character, human decency, and on-the-field skills will be found to replace Steve Largent."

SUPER BOWL BLUEPRINT

When Mike Holmgren arrived in Seattle in 1999 amid the pomp and circumstance that accompanies any man trumpeted as a savior, the Super Bowl champion coach was expected to work the same magic that he had in Green Bay. And while he did coax an overachieving team into the playoffs in his first season in Seattle, the whole process of building a championship-caliber club took a lot longer than fans hoped it would or the cocksure coach thought it would.

But it did happen. In his seventh season in Seattle, Holmgren did indeed lead the Seahawks to the first Super Bowl appearance in the 30 years of the franchise's existence. It was easily the crowning achievement of a team that had muddled along forever as the epitome of medi-Hawk-rity.

In 29 years the Seahawks had sniffed the Super Bowl just once—in 1983, when they lost to the Los Angeles Raiders in the AFC Championship Game. And until 2005, they had not even won a playoff game in 20 years.

The 2005 season was a culmination of a disjointed building process that didn't really begin until Holmgren's second season in Seattle. This process ended only after he was stripped of general manager duties and owner Paul Allen was forced to choose between Holmgren and team president Bob Whitsitt.

Toward the end of the 2005 season, Holmgren admitted to reflecting on how long it took to make the Seahawks a Super Bowl team.

"Thinking back to my first press conference, when I said my goal was to get the team to the Super Bowl, I think if I hadn't said that, you guys would have been disappointed with me," the coach said. "I think most guys come in, and that's their goal. The timetable is a different thing. The timetable, depending on any number of things, that changes. Sometimes it changes so you're not even the guy anymore."

When Holmgren arrived in 1999, he was charged with turning around a franchise that had been the definition of mediocre under Dennis Erickson, who was 31–33 in four seasons. With Jon Kitna at quarterback, Holmgren finessed a playoff appearance out of the Seahawks in 1999 before he began to assemble the hand-picked offense that would eventually become the league's best.

In 2000 Holmgren drafted Shaun Alexander and tackle Chris McIntosh in the first round and Darrell Jackson in the third. In 2001 he traded for quarterback Matt Hasselbeck and drafted receiver Koren Robinson and guard Steve Hutchinson. In 2002 he completed his offensive makeover by picking tight end Jerramy Stevens in the first round.

The offense had its growing pains. McIntosh, bothered by a neck injury, played in just 24 games before he was released in 2003. Hasselbeck clashed with Holmgren in his first season and was benched for Trent Dilfer, who was 4–0 as a spot starter in 2001, to begin the 2002 season. Robinson fell prey to the demons of alcoholism and could not exorcize them, despite repeated chances given to him by Holmgren; the mercurial receiver was let go before the Super Bowl season after four tumultuous years. Stevens, who had a long rap sheet when he joined the Seahawks, continued to screw up through his first two years before finally showing some maturity and dedication in 2005, when he posted his best season.

The offense began to hit its stride in the second half of the 2002 season, after Dilfer had been knocked out for the season with an Achilles injury and Hasselbeck had reassumed command of the offense. Hasselbeck led Seattle to five wins in the final nine games and turned into the quarterback Holmgren had foreseen when he had acquired the passer from the Green Bay Packers the previous year. No longer fighting Holmgren's coaching, Hasselbeck became a legitimate NFL starter and secured his place as Seattle's starting

LARGENT'S NFL RECORDS

At the time of his retirement, Largent held six major NFL receiving records. As the NFL turned into a passing league, Jerry Rice and half a dozen others surpassed all of Largent's marks over the next decade. His records (and where he ranked after 2006):

Most receptions—819 (13th)
Most consecutive games with a reception—177 (fourth)
Most receiving yards—13,089 (ninth)
Most touchdown receptions—100 (seventh)
Most seasons with 50 or more receptions—10 (tied for sixth)
Most seasons with 1,000 receiving yards—8 (tied for fourth)

quarterback as he threw for 300 yards or more four times, twice setting the team record for yards in a game (427 and 449), and had 15 touchdown passes.

From that season on, Hasselbeck steadily grew into one of the league's elite quarterbacks. He went to the Pro Bowl in 2003 and probably should have gone in 2004, but his receivers sabotaged him with dropped passes all season long. Hasselbeck led the Seahawks to the playoffs in both 2003 and 2004, where they agonizingly lost both times.

In 2004 their season ended when Bobby Engram couldn't make a difficult catch of Hasselbeck's fourth-down pass in the end zone, leading to a 27–20 loss to the St. Louis Rams. In 2003 Hasselbeck dueled his former mentor, Brett Favre, in a playoff game against the Green Bay Packers at Lambeau Field. The game went to overtime, and after the Seahawks won the coin toss, Hasselbeck showed the bravado that had been three years in the making when he told his old Packers friends and the referee (not knowing the referee's microphone would broadcast it to the world), "We want the ball, and we're gonna score!" A few plays later, Al Harris returned an intercepted pass from Hasselbeck for the winning touchdown, sending the Seahawks to another agonizing postseason defeat and leaving them winless in the playoffs since 1984.

But they had turned into a perennial playoff team, a transition due largely to the emergence of Hasselbeck as a Pro Bowl quarterback.

"In Green Bay, we were able to get to the Super Bowl in five [years]," Holmgren said. "I've thought of the differences in the timetable, and one of the things was settling in with your quarterback. That's one thing. That might be as important as anything. Sometimes the coach, in an organization that you're new to, it's just kind of tough and you've got to get things in order before you start to go."

The Seahawks didn't really start to go until after Holmgren was forced to surrender his role as general manager before the 2003 season. He also fired his entire defensive staff and brought in old friend Ray Rhodes to run a more aggressive defense. Coincidence or not, that became the first time in four years the team drafted a defensive player in the first round. In the three previous drafts, Holmgren had used five first-round selections on offensive players. Then, with Bob Ferguson sitting as the new GM in 2003, the team picked cornerback Marcus Trufant. In 2004 it selected defensive tackle Marcus Tubbs. Suddenly—after four years of patching together a defense with aging defenders such as John Randle, Chad Eaton, and Levon Kirkland—the Seahawks were building a defense the same way they had constructed their offense.

It all came together in 2005—somehow. In February the team was in danger of losing its coach and its three best offensive players. Allen acted fast, firing Whitsitt, who had been at odds with Holmgren for years, so Holmgren would stay. Then, thanks to the return of contract negotiator Mike Reinfeldt, the team managed to re-sign Hasselbeck and franchise left tackle Walter Jones to lucrative long-term deals before they became free agents, which allowed the Seahawks to retain Alexander with the franchise-player designation. Then the team made another big move, hiring Tim Ruskell as team president.

Ruskell, a longtime personnel expert with the Tampa Bay Buccaneers and Atlanta Falcons, immediately began to improve the Seahawks. He remade half the defense, adding 10 players on that side of the ball, and brought in receiver Joe Jurevicius, a big target who had the championship experience and work ethic Ruskell sought. Almost every move paid off, and Ruskell received praise all year long for his quick fix of a defense that had been the Seahawks' Achilles' heel in the previous two playoff seasons.

The Seahawks opened the 2005 season with a 2–2 record, giving no sign they were about to become the NFC's Super Bowl representative. But they soon established themselves as the best team in their conference as they rattled off a franchise-record 11 straight wins and finished with a team-record 13 victories, the league's top-scoring offense and top-sacking defense, the league MVP (Alexander), and a team-record-tying seven Pro Bowl players (six on offense).

Alexander put together one of the best seasons in NFL history, leading the league with 1,880 rushing yards and setting the league record with 28 touchdowns (a mark that was quickly overcome by San Diego's LaDainian Tomlinson, who scored 31 times in 2006).

The Seahawks lost out on the Lombardi Trophy in one of the most controversial Super Bowls ever played (see chapter 8), but Holmgren had finally given Seattle a Super Bowl team.

When the Seahawks beat the Carolina Panthers in the NFC Championship Game on Sunday, January 22, 2006, Alexander summed up the journey under Holmgren: "We've come a long way. It's taken five years to put this group together, and we're happy where we are."

THE BAD

STRIKE 3: PATERA'S OUT

It all fell apart in 1982. After four years of steady growth, the Seahawks suddenly had regressed under Jack Patera. Back-to-back losing seasons and another poor start in 1982, coupled with a PR nightmare and a league-wide strike, led the Nordstrom family to fire the franchise's first coach and try again.

Using his old-school discipline and imaginative play-calling, Patera had nurtured the Seahawks into winners by their third season. But after a pair of 9–7 years in 1978 and 1979, they had slipped to 4–12 in 1980 and 6–10 in 1981, with a 10-game losing streak over those two seasons that stands as the longest in team history. After an 0–2 start in 1982, the Nordstroms decided it was time for a change. They fired both Patera and general manager John Thompson and temporarily replaced Patera with Mike McCormack, the team's new director of football operations.

"We have been disappointed at our lack of progress on the football field the past years, and that is the sole reason for the dismissal," Elmer Nordstrom told reporters on October 14, 1982. "It became apparent in our early-season performance that things hadn't turned around."

Before the 1982 season, Patera had promoted third-year veteran Dave Krieg to starting quarterback ahead of longtime starter Jim Zorn, and the Seahawks had lost their first two games, 21–7 to Cleveland and 23–21 at Houston.

Patera and Thompson also had made a very controversial move by waiving starting receiver Sam McCullum before the season. Seattle players signed a petition accusing management of cutting McCullum because he was the team's union representative, and the union was threatening to strike. McCullum was one of the most popular players on the team and had been named the Seahawks' most valuable player after the 1980 season, even though statistically he was still playing second fiddle to Steve Largent. McCullum ended up back with the Minnesota Vikings, who had made him available in the expansion draft in 1976.

"Sam was outspoken. He tried to stand up, and they cut him," Krieg said. "That showed me the business side of it."

When NFL players did indeed vote to strike before Week 3, the Nordstrom ownership took stock of the franchise and unanimously decided it was time for a change. Among the considerations was the fact that the release of McCullum had created a public backlash by union supporters against the Nordstrom department store chain. Also, Patera had been arrested for drunken driving the week before the strike.

"The strike gave us a chance to reflect on what's been going on," John Nordstrom said on October 14. "We're committed to producing a winning team."

The strike lasted eight weeks, and when the players put their uniforms back on, McCormack reinstated Zorn as the starting quarterback. The Seahawks won four of the final seven games, finishing the disrupted season with a 4–5 record and failing to qualify for the AFC's eight-team, loser-out postseason tournament.

The Seahawks went 35–59 under Patera, whom Thompson had hired from the Vikings in January 1976. The Seahawks won just two games in their first season, but they improved to 5–9 in 1977 and had winning records in the next two years. In fact, in 1978 Patera was named coach of the year and Thompson was named executive of the year.

"We were a struggling franchise, yet we had some very interesting talent," receiver Steve Largent said. "We actually did exceedingly better than people anticipated us doing from Year 1."

However, the Seahawks still had not made the playoffs, and then they began to backslide when their rushing game fell off drastically in 1980 and 1981. They went from averaging 4.3 yards per carry in 1978 to 3.6 in 1981, from scoring a combined 52 rushing touchdowns in 1978 and 1979 to just 27 in 1980 and 1981. And the defense had not improved appreciably, giving up an average of at least 344 yards per game in every season but 1980 (the team went 4–12 that season largely because the offense didn't help at all, scoring just 291 points).

The team's scouting department had long been criticized, and Thompson and Patera had made some questionable moves—such as drafting defensive tackle Steve Niehaus with the second overall pick in 1976 and trading away the second pick, and thus the rights to running back Tony Dorsett, in 1977. Niehaus, who was hindered by a bad shoulder, was traded to Minnesota for aging defensive end Carl Eller and a draft pick in 1979. Dorsett, of course, went on to become a Hall of Fame player for the Dallas Cowboys, while the Seahawks failed to generate much of a ground game behind linemen Steve August and Tom Lynch, two of the four guys they obtained with picks acquired in the Dorsett deal. The bottom line: the Seahawks just weren't good enough on either line or in the offensive backfield.

Patera knew it, but he thought the Nordstroms had planned to give him time to turn it around. However, a confluence of events conspired against him, and he learned his time was up while on a fishing trip during the strike.

"It was really unfortunate what the Seahawks did with that strike," Largent said. "It took us a while to recover. That was a little unsettling for everybody. When you lose a coach, it's not an easy thing."

Amid the somewhat promising finish to the 1982 season, the Seattle players signed a petition asking ownership to retain McCormack as coach for the 1983 season. McCormack, who had coached the Baltimore Colts for two years before coming to Seattle, had told media when he took over for Patera that he was doing so only because the owners had asked him to and that he preferred to stay in the front office. He said he was flattered by the players' vote of confidence.

In the end, McCormack was named president and general manager, and he then found the coach who would take the Seahawks to the playoffs the very next season. His name, of course, was Chuck Knox.

THEY SHOULDA PASSED ON THESE GUYS

The Seahawks' most successful seasons have been accomplished using the arms of unheralded quarterbacks, guys the franchise has found in places like Cal Poly-Pomona, "now-defunct" Milton, Central Washington, and the Green Bay Packers bench.

But there was a period during which the powers that be at Seahawks headquarters thought they needed to find a passer with pedigree, a first-round draft pick with a rocket arm who could single-handedly beat teams the way division rivals John Elway and Dan Fouts used to beat the Seahawks.

Thus, Seattle blew three first-round picks in five years on quarterbacks who, as it turned out, could neither throw nor win. Once these guys got on the field, it made fans long for the days of Jim Zorn and Dave Krieg. And when they got off the field for good, fans eventually were happy to see less-heralded quarterbacks like Jon Kitna and Matt Hasselbeck take the snaps.

Krieg replaced Zorn, and Hasselbeck replaced Kitna, but in between Krieg and Kitna came a string of forgettable first-round flops. The Seahawks always seemed to be looking for an upgrade over Krieg, an overachiever whose inconsistency led him to the bench on more than one occasion. When Seattle spent first-round draft choices on Kelly Stouffer and Dan McGwire, it was obvious the team was serious about replacing Krieg once and for all.

The first move came in 1988, when the team tried to trade Kenny Easley to the Phoenix Cardinals for Stouffer, who had sat out the 1987 season in a contract dispute after the Cardinals had drafted him in the first round. Easley failed a physical and the Seahawks ended up giving the Cardinals a first-round pick in the

HOLD THAT THOUGHT

Dave Krieg had one criticism of Hall of Fame player Steve Largent: "Largent made [Tony] Romo look like a Hall of Fame holder. He'd drop the ball and have to pick it up and run. I don't know what he was doing. Worst holder ever."

1989 draft and two fifth-rounders. It still stands as one of the worst deals the Seahawks have ever made.

As linebacker Dave Wyman said, "I would pick Dave Krieg 100 times out of 100 to lead me into battle over Kelly Stouffer."

Stouffer failed to supplant Krieg in three seasons. His only significant action came in 1988 when Krieg was knocked out with a shoulder injury in Week 3. Stouffer replaced Jeff Kemp at halftime of a 38–7 loss to San Francisco the next week and started the next six games, going 3–3. He did provide one very memorable moment in a 20–19 loss in New Orleans, throwing a touchdown pass on the same play he was knocked down with a broken nose.

That six-game stint was the longest Stouffer could muster while Krieg was still in town. The Seahawks, led by president Tom Flores, were so unimpressed that they invested yet another first-round pick in a quarterback in 1991. But instead of taking the guy they should have grabbed, a country bumpkin named Brett Favre, they used the 16th overall pick on the 6'8" brother of a baseball star.

The selection of Dan McGwire—brother of slugger Mark McGwire—was really made by owner Ken Behring, who apparently was eager to get rid of Krieg because he held the NFL record for fumbles.

Paul Moyer, who was an assistant coach at the time, said, "I remember Tom Flores walked in, motioned to Chuck, and Ken Behring was there. They all left the war room. They came back, and you could see—it was written all over Chuck's face—he was not happy. He didn't look mad, he just looked like, 'It's over.'"

Knox refused to perform his usual function of announcing the first-round pick to the media. And then he pulled aside his coaches and presciently told them, "Boys, coach your butts off this year because there's a good chance this is it."

Wyman said McGwire was a nice guy, "but you just watched him in practice, and you thought, 'No way. Not even close.' He wasn't anywhere near being an NFL quarterback. That was the end of Chuck. That was the end of the team for a while."

Krieg remained the starter in 1991, although a broken thumb in the season opener sidelined him for six weeks. That seemed to be a chance for one of the young quarterbacks to prove his mettle. But Knox eschewed Stouffer and McGwire and started the veteran Kemp for five games. And, just as he had foreseen, Knox was fired after the team finished 7–9.

Flores replaced Knox as coach and let Krieg leave in free agency so Stouffer and McGwire could fight it out for the starting gig. Stouffer won, but he lasted just four games before suffering a shoulder injury. McGwire lasted just one game before going down with a broken hip. That left the reins of the worst offense in Seahawks history to Stan Gelbaugh, who proceeded to lose all eight starts. But he apparently was better than Stouffer, who was benched for the final four games despite being healthy. During that 2–14 season, the three quarterbacks completed a league-low 48.3 percent of their passes, threw for just nine touchdowns and 23 interceptions, and tallied a putrid passer rating of 48.9.

So, after spending first-round picks in 1989 and 1991 on quarterbacks, what did the Seahawks do in 1993? Draft a quarterback, of course. With the second pick in the draft. That might not have been so bad if the Seahawks had been able to get Drew Bledsoe, the big thrower from the other side of the state (Washington State University). But the Seahawks had aced themselves out of the top pick in the draft by beating New England, which ended up with the top pick and Bledsoe. So the Seahawks went with the other highly rated "passer."

Coming off an incredible three seasons as Notre Dame's quarterback, Rick Mirer immediately stepped in as Seattle's starter. And he wasn't half bad in the first year, setting NFL records for completions, attempts, and yards by a rookie quarterback.

"In 1993 Rick was probably better for our team than Drew Bledsoe would have been because he could run and scramble a little bit. He was a pretty good leader," Moyer said.

Of course, it was all downhill from there as Mirer proved to be a poor fit in Flores's go-deep philosophy. After becoming the third rookie quarterback since 1970 to start every game, Mirer never played a complete season after 1993. And he impressed only by the way he regressed, never coming close to even the substandard 56.4 completion percentage of his rookie year.

As poor a fit as Mirer was for Flores's downfield attack, he was just as inappropriate as the passer in the spread offense Dennis Erickson brought to the Seahawks in 1995. By the end of 1996, Erickson had turned to John Friesz as his quarterback.

Rick Mirer was one of the Seahawks' several high-drafted quarterbacks that didn't pan out in the late 1980s and early 1990s.

By then, Stouffer and McGwire were long gone. Stouffer was let go after the 1992 season, with just 16 starts in five seasons since the Seahawks had sent three draft picks to the Cardinals for him. McGwire had even less to show for his time in Seattle, starting just five games and throwing just two touchdown passes in four seasons.

Unlike those two, the Seahawks managed to salvage something out of their third bust of a quarterback, sending Mirer and a fourth-round pick to Chicago for the 11th pick in the 1997 draft—a selection that the Seahawks parlayed into cornerback Shawn Springs.

Of course, Flores had nothing to do with that move. He had been fired after presiding over the three most pathetic years in team history, a stretch that saw the team go 14–34. Meanwhile, Krieg—the guy Flores never could replace—went on to start for four other teams from 1992 to 1998. And the Seahawks didn't make the playoffs again until 1999, when Mike Holmgren arrived and got the most out of Kitna, an undrafted diamond in the rough many likened to the overachieving Krieg.

"You look at the first-round draft picks we used on quarterbacks during that stretch there, and it's a shame," defensive tackle Joe Nash said. "Dave Krieg played seven more years, and he left because Ken Behring didn't like that Dave held the NFL record for fumbles."

In the end, there is no reason to wonder why the Seahawks were so bad from 1991 through 1996 (36–60): they dumped a winning quarterback and wasted three first-round picks in five years on quarterbacks they should have passed on.

A HOUSE DIVIDED: BOB WHITSITT VS. MIKE HOLMGREN

In January 2005 Paul Allen's Seahawks franchise was at a crossroads. It had just been ousted from the first round of the playoffs for the second consecutive season, and the owner was faced with deciding the direction of his team—on the field and off—for the next few years. It came down to a choice between his two feuding chiefs, coach Mike Holmgren and president Bob Whitsitt.

Allen chose to keep the coach, so on January 14, the owner fired Whitsitt, his longtime friend and sports executive who had been the Seahawks president since 1997 and who also had recently been removed from managing Allen's Portland Trail Blazers.

Although it was widely known that Holmgren and Whitsitt did not get along, Allen said that played no part in his decision. In a conference call with reporters the day he fired Whitsitt, Allen said, "This isn't about particular interpersonal dynamics. I have to look at the whole landscape. I just felt this was the decision I had to make."

But Allen had become aware of the dysfunctional dynamics of Whitsitt and the Seahawks' football people. The relationship between Whitsitt and Holmgren had deteriorated steadily since the president had hired the coach in 1999.

Holmgren came to Seattle on the promise that he would be in complete control of the football operation of the team. Upon his hire, he received the titles of executive vice president, general manager, and coach. But Holmgren's personnel moves over his first four seasons did not yield positive results. After a surprise playoff appearance in 1999, the team went 6–10, 9–7, and 7–9 over the next three years, and Holmgren found himself with the same record (31–33) that Dennis Erickson had assembled before Whitsitt replaced him with Holmgren. So, after the 2002 season, Allen and Whitsitt asked Holmgren to yield his personnel control and to focus on coaching the team.

Holmgren did not like the idea and considered leaving the team, but he felt he had built a solid foundation and an offense that was set to make a mark in the NFL. Besides, many of the people Holmgren had brought from Green Bay were still in the front office, and he would still have a say in the way things were done. So he agreed to give up control.

Bob Ferguson was hired as the new general manager, but he was little more than a glorified scout, a yes man, and a rambling PR mouthpiece in a Hawaiian shirt. While Ferguson said much about nothing, Whitsitt took the real power of a GM for himself. Whitsitt learned how to negotiate contracts from Mike Reinfeldt,

RUN-N-SHOOT YOURSELF IN THE FOOT

In 1990 coach Chuck Knox and offensive coordinator John Becker decided to change the offense to the run-n-shoot, a ball-control style that features short passes out of four-receiver formations. The Seahawks practiced the offense during the off-season and throughout training camp, and then they were shut out 17–0 in the season opener in Chicago. Knox immediately scrapped the offense and went back to the pro set the Seahawks had used in the previous seven seasons.

Holmgren's administrative vice president in charge of contracts and the salary cap. Then Whitsitt decided he could do the job himself, so in 2004 he told Reinfeldt he was going to cut his salary in half, reportedly from $500,000 to $250,000. Already feeling handcuffed by Whitsitt when trying to negotiate long-term deals with franchise offensive tackle Walter Jones and others, Reinfeldt quit, leaving Whitsitt as the Seahawks' main contract negotiator. That brought the silent power struggle between Whitsitt and Holmgren to a crescendo.

"He [Reinfeldt] is a good man. And a good football man," Holmgren told *The Seattle Times* in January 2005, just before Whitsitt was fired. "Mike's talented. Mike's good. And when you start losing good men, something's wrong."

Whitsitt—known as "Trader Bob" for the wheeling and dealing he had done while running the NBA's Trail Blazers and Seattle SuperSonics—mistakenly assumed he knew how to negotiate big contracts in the NFL, and he became the laughingstock of the league in the 2004 off-season when he essentially bargained against himself and overpaid Grant Wistrom by at least $6 million. The Seahawks were desperate for a pass-rushing defensive end, and they had struck out on Jevon Kearse on the first day of free agency. But they immediately got Wistrom to Seattle for a visit, and when Whitsitt made his offer, the former St. Louis Ram jumped at it.

According to sources, this is how the deal went down: Whitsitt made the mistake of making the first offer and suggesting a deal with a $12 million signing bonus. Tom Condon, one of the best representatives in the business, knew Wistrom was not a premier pass rusher who could command the $16 million bonus Kearse had received from the Philadelphia Eagles. Rather, Condon had hoped to get as much as $8 million for Wistrom, who had made his name as a hustling, hard-working overachiever. So Condon obviously had to be thrilled to hear Whitsitt's offer, and the agent immediately tried to get more by countering with a request for $16 million. They settled on $14 million, which at the time was the largest signing bonus ever paid by the Seahawks. Whitsitt and Wistrom both took grief for the six-year, $33 million deal over the next year as Wistrom missed seven games because of injuries.

Whitsitt also overpaid cornerback Bobby Taylor and defensive tackle Cedric Woodard. Coming off an ankle injury, Taylor left Philadelphia for Seattle's four-year deal worth almost $12 million. Woodard, who had done nothing before he started 12 games in 2003, got a five-year deal worth $15 million. Both players failed to live up to the value of their contracts and were cut after the 2004 season.

Player acquisitions weren't Whitsitt's only failing. He had become a polarizing figure around the Seahawks headquarters, constantly alienating the football people and other team employees by excluding them in decisions and creating a divisive atmosphere.

Former player and coach Paul Moyer, who now works for the team as a broadcaster, said: "It was weird. It was a house divided: the Whitsitt camp and the Holmgren camp. It was controlled by fear. It was not a comfortable, cohesive organization."

Whitsitt's most public show of disrespect for the Seahawks and their history came when he apparently decided Jerry Rice should wear No. 80, the number the receiver had worn throughout his spectacular career. The Seahawks had obtained Rice in a trade with the Oakland Raiders in October 2004, and Whitsitt immediately called Hall of Famer Steve Largent to ask if Rice could wear Largent's Seahawks number, which had been retired in 1995 when the best and most popular Seahawk ever was inducted into the Hall of Fame.

Whitsitt made it sound to Largent like Rice wanted to wear the number, so Largent told Whitsitt to have Rice call him. On the other end, Whitsitt told Rice that Largent wanted him to wear his number. Whitsitt actually dialed Largent and handed the phone to Rice. Largent graciously allowed Rice to wear the number, but he warned him to prepare for a possible backlash from longtime fans who wouldn't want to see anyone else wear No. 80.

Indeed, the public outcry was so vehement that Rice's wife called a Bay Area newspaper to explain what had happened so her husband would not be vilified. Through the entire drama, Whitsitt never did admit that he had created the snafu himself. Later, Largent expressed annoyance over Whitsitt's disingenuous tactics that put both Largent and Rice—two of the greatest receivers in NFL history—in uncomfortable positions.

That episode surely came as no surprise to Holmgren, who after the 2004 season told *The Seattle Times* that Whitsitt had not lived up to promises he had made when he hired Holmgren.

"I was told some things when I got here," Holmgren said. "And that hasn't been the way it was. It just hasn't. I view myself as an honest person, and there's just been too much dishonesty. Just out and out flat lying. I think that's absurd, and I just don't get it."

WHERE DID THEY GO?

Some of the Seahawks' best players were not allowed to finish their careers in Seattle.

Player	Where he went
QB Dave Krieg	Kansas City in Plan B free agency in 1992
RB Curt Warner	L.A. Rams in Plan B in 1990
CB Dave Brown	Traded to Green Bay in 1987
FS Eugene Robinson	Traded to Green Bay in 1996
DE Jacob Green	San Francisco in Plan B in 1992

Holmgren also had become frustrated that he could communicate with Allen only through Whitsitt.

"There was a conduit to deal with [Allen] instead of talking to him directly," Holmgren said. "And you're not always sure if the message was getting across because of the communication thing."

Whitsitt was letting Holmgren's carefully crafted organization crumble to pieces around them. Whitsitt had chased away Reinfeldt and had done nothing to try to keep vice president Ted Thompson and college scouting director Scot McCloughan, who both ended up leaving after the 2004 season. In addition, Whitsitt had done nothing to try to keep any of the 16 players who were to become unrestricted free agents after the season. That number included the three best players on the team—Jones, quarterback Matt Hasselbeck, and running back Shaun Alexander.

It was so bad that Holmgren decided he could not continue to work with Whitsitt. So after the Seahawks lost to the St. Louis Rams in the playoffs to end the season, Holmgren went to Allen and told him he was considering leaving the team.

Allen knew then he would have to make a choice between his loyal longtime sports manager and his frustrated Super Bowl–caliber coach. And the decision paid off in 2005, when Holmgren led the Seahawks to their first Super Bowl.

Late in the 2005 season, Holmgren summed up his time in Seattle: "My good fortune is that, along the way, when I had the choice, I decided to stay, and when it appeared not to be my choice, Mr. Allen decided to stick with me. It's been an interesting seven years."

THE UGLY

NO OFFENSE, TEZ

How does a team go from a perennial playoff contender to one of the worst teams in NFL history?

Just get rid of the best coach and quarterback in team history and place a couple dozen players on injured reserve. That's what the Seahawks did in 1992 when they put together the worst season in franchise history despite having the best defense they had ever had and the NFL's defensive player of the year, Cortez Kennedy.

After the 1991 season, the Seahawks parted ways with coach Chuck Knox, who had led the team to the playoffs in four of his nine seasons, and club president Tom Flores took over as coach. Then Flores let veteran quarterback Dave Krieg go so former first-round picks Kelly Stouffer and Dan McGwire could vie for leadership of the offense. It was all downhill from there as the Seahawks set an NFL record for fewest points scored in a 16-game season and finished with a 2–14 record, the worst season in team history (the Hawks went 2–12 in their expansion season of 1976).

The 1992 club was the most bipolar pairing of offense and defense in franchise history. But bad offense trumped good defense, creating one of the worst teams in the history of the NFL. An ESPN.com poll of readers ranked the 1992 Seahawks as the 10th-worst team in NFL history, and the website itself put them down for the 13th worst in league history.

"That was ugly," admitted Paul Moyer, who coached the secondary that season. "It was the most inept offense in the history of the NFL."

Indeed it was. The offense set an NFL record for fewest points scored in a 16-game season (140), along with nine other team records no offense would want to be part of. The offense was so bad that defensive end Greg Townsend said he wished his Raiders could play against it every week.

Everything that could go wrong did. Stouffer won the starting quarterback job out of training camp, but a shoulder injury knocked him out after four games and he was benched for the final four. His

> ### DID YOU KNOW...
>
> In a 24–21 overtime loss to Denver in October 1989, a punt by Ruben Rodriguez netted minus-2 yards...inside the Kingdome.

worst game included four interceptions and a fumble in a 24–14 loss to Kansas City at the Kingdome. (The winning quarterback? Dave Krieg, who had signed with the Chiefs after the Seahawks had told him they no longer wanted him.)

McGwire started just one game before a broken hip sidelined him. That left things in the hands of journeyman Stan Gelbaugh, who lost all eight games he started. In all, the three quarterbacks completed a league-low 48.3 percent of their passes, with just nine touchdowns and 23 interceptions.

"Dan McGwire was a horrible quarterback," Moyer said. "Stan Gelbaugh would have been a second-team World League player. McGwire just couldn't play football."

Neither could many other Seahawks in a season in which they put 21 players on injured reserve. Top receiver Brian Blades missed 10 games after hurting his shoulder in the season opener. Fullback John L. Williams was one of many players who played hurt all season. Despite injuries to his foot, ankle, and fingers, he led the team with 74 catches for 556 yards and rushed for 339 yards. His ability to play through the injuries inspired tailback Chris Warren, a first-year starter who was the lone bright spot as he became the second Seahawks player to rush for 1,000 yards in a season (1,017).

The offensive line was banged up and gave up a league-high and franchise-record 67 sacks. Rookie right tackle Ray Roberts was so bad early in the season that Raiders defensive end Howie Long told reporters after a 19–0 win, "It was like guys at Baskin-Robbins lining up for a ticket to get a shot at him."

No quarterback, no receivers, no healthy linemen. And no coaching. Led by first-year coordinator Larry Kennan, the Seahawks threw the ball when they should have run it and ran it when they should have thrown it. The entire offense was a mess.

Linebacker Dave Wyman remembers a November loss to the Raiders in Los Angeles in which the Seahawks defense held the Raiders to less than 200 yards. But the offense could do nothing, and Seattle lost 20–3. Wyman said the offense would end up with fourth down and 10 yards to go or fourth-and-25 or fourth-and-30. "It was never fourth-and-two or fourth-and-three."

Of course, all of those fourth downs translated into Rick Tuten setting a team record for most punts (108) that still stands. And second-year kicker John Kasay didn't help matters by making a mere 14-of-22 field-goal attempts—the second-worst percentage (.636) in the NFL. He missed three field goals in Pittsburgh in a game the Seahawks lost 20–14.

Wyman's running joke all year was that he never got to sit long enough to finish a cup of Gatorade because the defense always had to go right back on the field. But Wyman also credited Flores with keeping the team together.

"Flores probably did the best coaching job of his life," Wyman said. "There were never any fights.... It never occurred to me to get pissed off."

The defensive guys had every reason to be upset. For the third straight season, they set a club record for fewest yards allowed. They were the league's 11th-ranked unit (fourth against the pass), and defensive tackle Cortez Kennedy was the NFL defensive player of the year. And all it got them was a 2–14 record.

Moyer said the defensive coaches cut it loose and had fun because expectations were so low. So while Kennedy dominated

Cortez Kennedy was about the only bright spot for Seattle during a dismal 1992 season.
Photo courtesy of Getty Images.

the interior, Moyer put safety Eugene Robinson in position to make plays, too. The result was a team-best 94 tackles and seven interceptions and Robinson's first Pro Bowl appearance.

Kennedy, meanwhile, was a monster in the middle. Despite facing constant double- and triple-team blocking throughout the season, he led the Seahawks with 14 sacks, four forced fumbles, 76 solo tackles, and a team-record 28 tackles for loss. He was not only the best player on the team, he was also the best defensive player in the league, joining Kenny Easley (1984) as the only Seahawks to be so honored.

"It was probably one of the most fun seasons I've played in because playing linebacker behind Cortez Kennedy was so much fun," said Wyman, who was in his sixth and final season with Seattle in 1992.

"He was such a good teammate—humble, funny, a phenomenal athlete," Wyman said. "You look at him and go, 'That guy is a short, fat little lard.' But he would wipe out three guys on one play. He was so good. When he couldn't make a play, he was going to make it so you could."

Kennedy carried a defense that was hit by injuries of its own—Wyman and linebacker Terry Wooden missed time and linebacker Rufus Porter played hurt for most of the season—and the unit often kept the Seahawks in position to win (or lose by less than they should have).

But, as odd as it is to say, the Seahawks didn't lose enough. Their two wins came against the New England Patriots and then against the Denver Broncos in an overtime game on a Monday night. If the Seahawks had lost either game, they would have ended up with the number one pick in the 1993 draft and then taken local star quarterback Drew Bledsoe, who had made himself the top pro prospect during his junior year at Washington State University. Instead, the Seahawks ended up with the number two pick in the draft and settled for Rick Mirer, who lasted all of four seasons in Seattle.

Patrick Hunter was the guy to blame for the New England win; his goal-line interception saved Seattle's 10–6 victory at New England in the third week.

Gelbaugh was the one who engineered perhaps the most bittersweet victory in franchise history—the Monday night win over the Broncos that not only would prevent the Seahawks from winning the draft sweepstakes but also would be the final game for longtime broadcaster Pete Gross.

Before the game on November 30, 1992, the team inducted Gross into its Ring of Honor, and there was nary a dry eye in the Kingdome as Gross, who was suffering from terminal cancer, waved goodbye to the fans. The Seahawks then proceeded to play an inspired game. Blades, back after missing all but the first game because of a shoulder injury, caught the tying touchdown pass on the final play of regulation, and Kasay kicked the winning 32-yard field goal in overtime as the Hawks broke an eight-game losing streak with a 16–13 victory. Gross, who had been the only broadcaster in the team's 17-year history, died 52 hours later.

It was a tragic end to perhaps the most disheartening season in team history.

FRANCHISE ON THE MOVE

When Ken Behring bought the Seahawks in 1988, he said he had no intention of moving them to his home state of California.

"You sure would not take a team out of a place where they sell out the stadium every week," he told reporters then. "The fans would kill you, and I wouldn't blame them."

In an interview with a Seattle TV station, he added: "I think Seattle is the greatest football city in the country. I would not even consider buying [the Seahawks] if for some reason they had to be moved."

But there was always the tingling feeling on the back of the necks of many fans that, if Behring could find a reason, he would indeed try to take the Seahawks south.

And after taking them south in the standings for eight years, Behring finally confirmed fans' fears in February 1996 when he announced he was moving the franchise to Los Angeles, which had just lost the Rams and Raiders the previous year.

Behring thought he had his handy reason, too, after a ceiling tile had fallen in the Kingdome in 1994 and forced the Seahawks to play their preseason games and three regular-season games at University of Washington's Husky Stadium. Behring claimed King County had failed to maintain the Kingdome as a "first-class facility," and he cited an alleged lack of structural integrity in the event of an earthquake. (That reasoning didn't sit well with anyone: he wanted to move the team from Seattle to Los Angeles to *escape* earthquakes?)

Behring had sought $170 million in renovations to the Kingdome, including the addition of luxury seats. But county officials and state legislators were preoccupied with the Mariners' new stadium and gave no heed to the NFL owner who had

DEATH AND DISASTER: THE WORST DAYS IN FRANCHISE HISTORY

- **January 20, 1976:** Lloyd W. Nordstrom, the Seahawks majority owner, dies of a heart attack while vacationing in Mexico.
- **April 1988:** Kenny Easley is diagnosed with kidney failure after taking a physical with the Phoenix Cardinals, an ailment that ends the career of the All-Pro safety.
- **December 2, 1992:** Team broadcaster Pete Gross dies of cancer, two days after he is inducted into the team's Ring of Honor.
- **December 1, 1994:** Defensive tackle Mike Frier is paralyzed during a car accident in which star running back Chris Warren is also a passenger and teammate Lamar Smith is the driver.
- **July 5, 1995:** Brian Blades's cousin, Charles, dies of a gunshot wound inflicted as the two struggle for the weapon at Blades's home in Plantation, Florida.
- **June 28, 1998:** Glenn Montgomery, a 31-year-old defensive tackle, dies of Lou Gehrig's disease in Houston.
- **August 30, 1999:** Defensive coordinator Fritz Shurmur, new coach Mike Holmgren's right-hand man and good friend, dies of liver cancer at age 67 in Green Bay.
- **April 27, 2003:** Quarterback Trent Dilfer's 5-year-old son, Trevin, dies of heart disease at a Stanford University children's hospital.

allowed his team to become one of the league's bottom feeders under his watch.

With one bad decision after another, Behring had turned a proud franchise into a perennial loser. He had hired Tom Flores to be team president, had personally chosen quarterback Dan McGwire in the 1991 draft against coach Chuck Knox's wishes, and then had fired Knox after the team went 7–9 that season. Then he had made Flores the coach even though many didn't think Flores—who had once coached the Raiders—was really up to the task of coaching again.

It turns out he wasn't. In Flores's first year, the Seahawks put together their worst season ever, going 2–14 and setting records for offensive futility. Then Flores and Behring used their first-round pick in 1993 on another quarterback, Rick Mirer. But he wasn't the solution, as the team went 6–10 in both 1993 and 1994, leading Behring to fire Flores and replace him as president with Behring's son, David. Then the Behrings hired Dennis Erickson to try to lead the franchise out of its three-season morass. He bumped the team to .500 in his first season, and then Behring made his move.

He announced the decision on February 2, and a few days later had his trucks hauling gear from the Seahawks headquarters in Kirkland, Washington, down to Anaheim, California, where he planned to set up shop and conduct off-season workouts. "I'm committed to Los Angeles," Behring told *The Los Angeles Times*. "I'm a Californian, and this is where I want to be."

Defensive tackle Joe Nash, who had played in over 200 games for the Seahawks since 1982, was still on the roster and received a letter from the front office notifying him of the move.

"It was really strange," Nash said. "I couldn't think of the Seahawks being anywhere else other than Seattle."

Paul Moyer, who played safety for the team from 1983 through 1989 and was an assistant coach from 1990 to 1994, remembered his reaction: "It was like, what did they just do? Can they do that?"

Dave Wyman, who had played linebacker from 1987 to 1992 before signing with Denver, said he was at former quarterback Dave Krieg's house and remembers calling in to a talk show. "I said, 'I think Ken Behring should leave town, but without the team.' It was so hard to have been a player there and see what was going on."

King County leaders tried to stop the team from moving with a temporary restraining order, but they were powerless because the lease with the Kingdome did not prohibit the Seahawks from training out of state.

While King County and state lawmakers tried using legal action to stop Behring from moving the team, NFL commissioner

Paul Tagliabue expressed his displeasure over the unsanctioned move.

"There is very serious concern on my part and among the ownership on the Seattle situation in terms of the Seahawks just picking up and seeming to relocate their practice facility to Southern California," Tagliabue told reporters. "The Seahawks are the NFL team in the Pacific Northwest, and there is an expectation among the ownership and on my part that they represent the league in every way possible in the Pacific Northwest."

Tagliabue had already seen two NFL franchises move in the past year, and the owners had just approved Art Modell's decision to move his franchise from Cleveland to Baltimore. After the Rams and Raiders had vacated Los Angeles the previous year, the owners—Behring included—had signed a resolution giving the league control of the L.A. market. So Tagliabue was unhappy with Behring's attempted end-around.

In late February King County officials met with Tagliabue in New York to discuss ways to keep the Seahawks in Seattle. Meanwhile, Behring began discussions with Bob Whitsitt about the possibility of Whitsitt's boss, Microsoft billionaire Paul Allen, purchasing the Seahawks.

But Behring was still intent on keeping the team in California. The Seahawks began off-season workouts in Anaheim on March 18, with 32 players reporting to the old school where the Rams used to be based. Conspicuously absent was star defensive tackle Cortez Kennedy, and David Behring obviously felt the team's best player was trying to show up ownership by his absence; Behring went into a tirade about how Kennedy was fat and lazy and not a team leader. Behring apparently realized the idiocy of insulting a five-time Pro Bowl player because the president apologized the next day, admitting he had spoken out of frustration.

Just three days after the Seahawks began workouts, Tagliabue threatened to fine Behring $500,000 if he did not move the team's off-season camp back to Kirkland. With negotiations under way to sell the team, Behring had the team back in Washington by the end of March.

It was the first good thing to happen to Seattle fans under Behring's ownership since the team had won the division title in his first year as owner. The next good thing came a month later, when Behring and Allen agreed on an exclusive 14-month purchase option. Allen reportedly paid $18 million for the option and the right to sign off on major franchise decisions over the next year.

But there were still hurdles to keeping the franchise in Seattle. Allen would not buy the team unless voters agreed to pay for a new stadium. And, because Allen owned the NBA's Portland Trail Blazers, the NFL had to eliminate its prohibition on owners possessing a team in more than one sport. NFL owners abolished the rule in a vote at their March 1997 meetings.

Then, on April 25, 1997, the Washington state legislature passed a funding plan for Seahawks Stadium, which called for the public to pay $300 million and Allen to provide $130 million plus any cost overruns. The legislature set a statewide vote for June 17, and the referendum barely passed, 51.1 to 48.9 percent.

With the new stadium on the way, Allen finished his purchase of the Seahawks in June 1997. Behring, who had bought the team for $80 million, reportedly sold it for $200 million. And everyone was happy the team was no longer in Behring's hands or in Los Angeles. It was in Seattle to stay.

BLADES'S TRIALS

Brian Blades was such a team leader and such a giving man that he was honored with the Steve Largent Award and named the Seahawks' Man of the Year in 1994.

They were honors earned through Blades's undying dedication to his team and his countless charitable endeavors in Seattle and South Florida—helping young children, paying for scholarships at his old high school, raising money for the United Negro College Fund, and holding holiday events for the underprivileged.

As charitable as he was, Blades was no angel. In 1989 two women had accused him of assault, and in 1991 he was arrested for drunken driving. He was known to party to excess when back home with his brother in South Florida, and he reportedly spent lavishly on cars and women. Despite his indiscretions, Blades was considered one of the NFL's good guys.

That is what made it such shocking news when Blades found himself the subject of a manslaughter case after the shooting death of his cousin in July 1995. On the evening of July 4, Brian's brother, fellow NFL player Bennie Blades, was having a dispute with the mother of one of his children. Brian had gone into his condominium in Plantation, Florida, to get his gun so he allegedly could scare the woman into leaving. Brian's older cousin, Charles, tried to intercede; and, in the struggle to possess the semiautomatic pistol, the weapon discharged and killed Charles.

On June 14, 1996, a jury found Brian Blades guilty of manslaughter. But 72 hours later, circuit judge Susan Lebow overturned the verdict and acquitted Blades, stating that the prosecution had not proven that Blades had acted negligently in the shooting. Thus, Blades escaped a prison sentence of at least five years and nine months.

But he could never escape the knowledge that he had helped cause the death of his cousin and best friend.

Brian Blades, named the Seahawks Man of the Year in 1994, appears in court during his manslaughter trial two years later.

"It's something I will never put behind me," Blades told reporters when training camp opened in July 1996, his first comments about the incident since it had happened a year before. "It was something I wouldn't wish on my worst enemy."

As he awaited trial, Blades was left to anguish over the events of that tragic night throughout the 1995 season. He dedicated that season to Charles, and he managed to focus on his game well enough to lead the Seahawks in receiving and record his fourth season with at least 1,000 receiving yards. He finished with a team-high 77 catches for 1,001 yards and four touchdowns in Dennis Erickson's first season as coach.

Asked whether he was surprised he played so well in 1995, Blades told reporters, "I wouldn't say I surprised myself. I just proved to myself I'm one of those players that can put everything behind him once he steps on the field and focuses on what he has to do."

But Blades couldn't keep the thoughts of what had happened and what was about to happen entirely out of his mind. "Toward the end of the season," he said, "I was drained, mentally and physically, because of what I'd been through and what I was getting ready to go through."

As he prepared for his second season without Charles in his life, Blades said, "I just came back here [to Washington] concentrating on football, the same as last year. Once I get inside those white lines, I can't control what's on the outside. That's where my focus was last year, and that's where it's going to be this year."

But at age 31, Blades did not have nearly as successful of a season in 1996. He missed five games and finished with just 43 catches for 556 yards and two touchdowns. That was the beginning of the end for Blades, who caught just 45 passes over his final two seasons.

In his 11-year career with the Seahawks, the former second-round draft choice finished second to Steve Largent with 581 receptions and 7,620 yards. While he trailed Largent (819 receptions and 13,089 yards) in those and other categories, Blades did leave with the team record for receptions in a season—81 in 1994 and 80 in 1993 (since broken by Darrell Jackson with 87 in 2004).

FEWEST YARDS IN A GAME

The Seahawks hold the NFL record for fewest yards in a game. They netted minus-7 yards in a 24–0 loss to the Los Angeles Rams on November 4, 1979.

Yards	Team	Opponent	Date
minus-7	Seattle	L.A. Rams	Nov. 4, 1979
minus-5	Denver	Oakland	Sept. 10, 1967
14	Chicago Cardinals	Detroit	Sept. 15, 1940

He also was named to the Pro Bowl in 1989, when he caught 77 balls for 1,063 yards and five scores and was voted the Seahawks most valuable player.

For much of his career, Blades was the consummate professional on the field and off—helping his team win games and helping his communities raise their children. He was honored for both endeavors. But in 1995 this legacy of good deeds was tarnished by the blood of his cousin in one of the most tragic events in the history of the Seahawks.

1987—IT WAS GOOD, BAD, AND UGLY

SUPER BOWL: STRIKE THAT

Everything seemed set for the Seahawks in 1987. They had won their final five games of 1986 and just missed the playoffs despite a 10–6 record. They returned nearly every starter on offense and defense. They had fortified their defense in the draft with linebackers Tony Woods and Dave Wyman. And they had managed to overcome 37-1 odds to secure the rights to linebacker Brian Bosworth in the supplemental draft. With all of that in mind, many prognosticators were picking the Seahawks to represent the AFC in the Super Bowl.

But it didn't turn out nearly as well as anyone had hoped. From Bosworth's contentious contract negotiations to the NFL players' strike to a controversial loss in the playoffs to the unexpected loss of two of the team's best defenders to the eventual sale of the team to Ken Behring, 1987 became one of the most frustrating seasons in team history.

Bosworth was a distraction from the start, especially in the season-opening, 40–17 loss in Denver in which the rookie was the sole focus of the game. The Seahawks rebounded from that debacle to destroy Kansas City 43–14 at the Kingdome in Week 2. But then things shut down.

For the second time in six seasons, NFL players voted to strike as they sought concessions from the team owners: unrestricted free agency, guaranteed contracts for veterans, higher minimum salaries, and better pension and medical benefits. The players walked out before the third game, and owners were forced to cancel the contests that weekend.

But, unlike 1982, when the owners were unable to put together replacement teams during a seven-week strike, the league managed to field substitute squads in 1987. They took the field in Week 4 and played three games before the regular players gave up and returned to their teams.

The Seahawks managed to go 1–1 in the first two games, led by quarterback Bruce Mathison and wide receiver Jimmy Teal, as well as fullback Eric Lane, the Seahawks' former special-teams captain who had been cut that summer. Five regular players—Steve Largent, Fredd Young, Blair Bush, Jeff Kemp, and Norm Johnson—returned a day before the strike ended and just beat the Wednesday deadline to play in the fifth game of the season.

The return of Kemp and Largent assured the Seahawks of victory against the Detroit Lions' small-college-caliber secondary, and Seattle cruised to a 37–14 victory. Kemp, the backup to Dave Krieg who had not thrown a pass all season, completed 20 of 27 throws for 344 yards and four touchdowns.

Largent had a field day, setting team records with 15 catches for 261 yards and scored three touchdowns before he left with about nine minutes remaining in the third quarter. If he had not removed himself, he easily would have broken the NFL record of 18 catches in a game, which had been set by the Los Angeles Rams' Tom Fears in 1950.

"It was fun but embarrassing at the same time," Largent recalled. "I'm glad we got the win and got out of there. In the third quarter, I told [Coach] Chuck [Knox] I thought we had won and there was no reason for me to stay in the game. I wasn't there to pad my statistics. So he took me out."

That win proved to be vital in the Seahawks' push to the play-offs that season. If they had lost, they would have ended up in a five-way tie at 8–7 for the final wild-card spot and would not have made the playoffs because they had too many losses within the conference.

SEAHAWKS COACHING RECORDS

Seasons	Coach	Record	Pct.	Playoffs
1976–82*	Jack Patera	35–59	.372	None
1982	Mike McCormack	4–3	.571	None
1983–91	Chuck Knox	80–63	.559	3–4
1992–94	Tom Flores	14–34	.292	None
1995–98	Dennis Erickson	31–33	.484	None
1999–	Mike Holmgren	72–56	.563	3–4

*Patera was replaced by McCormack after two games in 1982.

Of course, the five players who crossed the picket line did not make many friends with the teammates they had left behind. Earlier that week at a team meeting at tight end Mike Tice's deli in Redmond, they had told their teammates of their intention to play.

"I didn't blame them," nose tackle Joe Nash said of the quintet, "but some did. There were guys that were upset about it, and it caused animosity that probably took years to work itself out."

"Enough time had expired," Largent said of the strike, which lasted 24 days. "I had told them I would sit out, but not forever. When guys like me came back, the negotiations seemed to pick up."

The rest of the players returned a day later, but missed the league-imposed deadline for being able to play that week.

The Seahawks got right back into the flow the next game, blowing out the Raiders 35–13 in Los Angeles. They won four of their first five games after the strike and managed to squeeze into the playoffs as a wild-card team. A loss in Kansas City prevented them from hosting the Houston Oilers, and they lost 23–20 in overtime at the Astrodome when an apparent interception by Fredd Young was ruled incomplete. The Seahawks played that game without running back Curt Warner (who sat out with an ankle injury).

That also was the last game Young or Kenny Easley played for the Seahawks, and it was the last game the team played under the ownership of the Nordstroms. The team tried to trade Easley in the off-season, only to find out he had a career-ending kidney disease. And Young forced a trade in August 1988 because he was unhappy that Bosworth was making more money than him.

The Nordstroms almost sold their majority interest in the team after the 1982 strike. They had put the franchise on the market in 1986 because they wanted to focus on their chain of department stores, and the huge public-relations hit they took during the 1987 strike probably gave them incentive to finally find a buyer. They sold the team to Behring in August 1988 for a reported $80 million.

News of the sale hit players hard because the Nordstrom family had always treated the team members so well. "They were phenomenal people...fantastic owners," Nash said.

Nash and safety Paul Moyer agreed the team atmosphere changed under Behring, who inherited the team just in time to see it claim its first AFC West title in 1988.

"The strike was almost the beginning of the downward spiral of the franchise," Moyer said. "The Nordstroms decided to sell the team mostly because of the strike. When Behring bought the team, it wasn't family anymore."

The good times were over. The players were miffed at their union leadership for failing again, and some were mad at their teammates for not sticking together. And eventually everyone would be unhappy with the way Behring ran the team into the ground over the next decade.

THE BOZ

Dave Krieg finds it fascinating—and a little ridiculous—that Brian Bosworth still receives so much attention nearly 20 years after his short but showy stint with the Seahawks.

"It's funny how people want to talk about a guy who was there for only two or three years," said Krieg, referring to Bosworth's

Brian Bosworth's short NFL career falls into the "more hype than substance" category.

appearance on *Monday Night Football* when the Seahawks played the Oakland Raiders in 2006.

Of course, the occasion for ESPN interviewing Bosworth that night was to relive one of the most infamous moments in NFL history—the play that branded Bosworth and eventually came to signify the failure of one of the most hyped players in NFL history. It's the indelible image of Bosworth's brief career: Bo Jackson carrying the rookie linebacker into the end zone during the running back's breakout performance on *Monday Night Football* in 1987.

If Bosworth had not been such a self-centered, outspoken, rebellious maverick—if he hadn't purposely tried to foster his image as a "modern day anti-hero"—that play on Monday night would not have meant nearly as much. But Bosworth was a national villain—a preening, blustering bad boy who had planned to use the NFL as a stepping-stone to the entertainment world, a loud-mouthed linebacker from Oklahoma who had turned Seattle into the Land of Boz.

The Boz didn't fit with the Seahawks, who were a largely anonymous franchise populated with understated players—Krieg, Steve Largent, Curt Warner, Jacob Green, Kenny Easley, Dave Brown—who spoke with their play more than with their voices.

"We were used to having a team, guys who played together," Krieg said. "Then you have a guy who was an individual. It was kind of a detriment to our team. He was a good guy, but football's a team sport and you can't put one person above the team. He was more hype than substance.

"It's like we brought in someone from a different family, adding a rich kid to a bunch of hardworking guys," Krieg added. "He brought a swagger to the team, but we already had guys like Kenny Easley who had credibility and had proven themselves. Bosworth talked about what he was going to do. Others had already done it."

Bosworth's bravado didn't dissuade Seahawks management, which was enamored with his size and speed. When the Seahawks, against 37-1 odds, won the lottery for the 1987 supplemental draft, they did not hesitate in expending a 1988 first-round pick on the talented but talkative linebacker. Even though Bosworth and his agent, Gary Wichard, warned the Seahawks not to select him, the franchise ignored them and secured the rights to one of the most controversial characters ever to enter the NFL.

At Oklahoma, the Boz was a legend—a two-time All-American and winner of the Butkus Award as college football's best linebacker, he also came in fourth in voting for the 1986 Heisman Trophy. But it all ended after that 1986 season when he was suspended for the Orange Bowl because he had tested positive for steroid use. Bosworth was kicked off the team after the season and thus made himself available in the NFL's supplemental draft in June 1987.

He warned the Seahawks not to take him. He wanted to go to a media mecca where he could market himself appropriately. His list of preferred cities included New York, Los Angeles, and Philadelphia.

When he was drafted by the Seahawks, he told reporters, "Seattle doesn't fit the mold I want to put myself in."

Apparently the mold fit when it paid more than $1 million per year because in the end Bosworth joined the Seahawks after they offered a 10-year deal worth $11 million.

The Seahawks remember their impressions when Bosworth arrived, sporting his signature bleached-blond buzz cut, earring, and wraparound sunglasses.

"Everyone was running around saying we got this great player," nose tackle Joe Nash said. "Next thing I know he's flying in on a helicopter, landing on the field."

Dave Wyman had been drafted by the Seahawks in the second round in 1987, and he figured to be the heir apparent to veteran Keith Butler. Then, on the day he was to graduate from Stanford, he was disappointed to read that the Seahawks had won the rights to Bosworth.

When he got to training camp, the Hawks added insult to injury by rooming him with the guy who was supposed to take his job. Wyman and Bosworth didn't get along at first—the understated Stanford man and the boisterous Boz. But they eventually became good friends.

"He understood I wasn't going to buy his bullshit. Once we got past that, he was a really good guy," Wyman said. "I stuck up for him because he had a lot of pressure. He would complain about the pressure. And I would say, 'Hey stupid, you set those expectations. [You] got paid $11 million. Why whine about it?'"

Nash agreed with most of the Seahawks' opinions that Bosworth was a talented player and good person. "Brian Bosworth was a super nice guy," Nash said. "The Boz was a different situation."

And it was the Boz who always showed up in public.

After his prolonged posturing against the Seahawks, his next run-in was with the NFL itself. Bosworth wanted to continue to wear No. 44, the number he had donned on his cutoff Oklahoma jerseys. But NFL rules stipulated linebackers must wear a number in the 50s or 90s. Wichard threatened to sue the NFL, saying the league was "hurting Brian and his career off the field." The Boz had several merchandising deals based on No. 44, and he had worn a No. 44 jersey for the shooting of "The Land of Boz" poster—the soon-to-be-infamous depiction of the Boz with a vampish "Dorothy" and a little boy (munchkin) with the Boz's blond buzz cut. In the end, Bosworth lost his challenge to the NFL and settled for No. 55, which he arrived at because it was No. 44 plus the $11 million value of his contract.

Then came the trash talking. Days before his first NFL game, at Denver's Mile High Stadium, Bosworth told reporters he was looking forward to playing against Pro Bowl quarterback John Elway, whom he also referred to as Mr. Ed (the horse of sitcom fame).

Bosworth said, "You very rarely get a chance to get a shot on somebody like that. I'm going to take as many and as hard of shots as I can get on him."

Asked if he meant to hurt Elway, Bosworth replied, "Yeah.... That's just the way I approach the game. It might cost us 15 yards for roughing, but I'm not going to pull off on him."

After those comments, the anti-Boz sentiment was in full bloom on game day at Mile High. Some of the Seahawks linemen found some Bosworth-bashing T-shirts and decided to have a little fun with the brash rookie.

"The linemen come strolling into the locker room wearing Boz Buster shirts, and Brian starts laughing," Wyman recalled. "He looks over at me and says, 'Those guys put money in my pocket.'"

Because, in one of the more brilliant marketing moves ever conceived, Bosworth had distributed the shirts through his company and sold them to Denver fans who were all fired up about him. It was a bonus that his own teammates had contributed to the coffers of 44 Boz, Inc.

"He was as business savvy as a 10-year vet," Wyman said. "It was kind of the whole Vince McMahon thing, where you get attention by people hating you."

In Denver, Bosworth got into the first of many uniform arguments with referees, who wanted him to take off the No. 44 stickers he was wearing on his helmet in protest of not being able to wear his college jersey number, which he had used to establish 44 Boz, Inc.

"It was just distracting," Nash said. "Here we are playing a game, and he's out there marketing himself."

Even Elway was distracted, having to call a timeout early in the game because Denver fans were taunting Bosworth so loudly. A few minutes later, Bosworth got his big hit on Elway as he ran for the sideline, and the linebacker taunted the quarterback with a primal scream. But Elway ignored the grandstanding rookie and went on to throw for 321 yards as the Broncos destroyed the Seahawks 40–17.

When the NFL players voted to strike after Week 2 of the 1987 season, Bosworth took advantage of the time off to—what else?—promote himself. As his teammates walked the picket lines for the next three weeks, Bosworth often was busy making appearances on *The Tonight Show*, *Good Morning America*, and other talk programs.

Six weeks after the Seahawks returned to the field, they hosted the Los Angeles Raiders on *Monday Night Football* in the infamous game. Bo Jackson, the Raiders' first-year star, had a national coming-out party at the Kingdome, rushing for 221 yards. He scored on a 91-yard run in which he outran Bosworth and the rest of the defense, and then in the third quarter Jackson made the play everyone remembers—carrying Bosworth into the end zone from the 2-yard line.

That surely would not have been the lasting snapshot of Bosworth's career if the linebacker had been able to play longer than just three years. In fact, he finished his rookie season with 81 tackles and was named to the NFL's all-rookie team. He capped that season with 17 tackles in the Seahawks' overtime wild-card loss to the Houston Oilers.

WEIGHT WATCHERS

Chuck Knox wanted defensive tackle Cortez Kennedy, who weighed over 300 pounds, to play at a specific weight, and the coach would do whatever it took to make sure Kennedy played at that weight. "Weigh-in was Friday morning," linemate Joe Nash said. "Tez would sit in a hot box Wednesday and Thursday. He'd get on the scale Friday, and they'd say, 'Close enough.' Come game time, he'd be back up to where he was before. So Chuck started bringing the scale to the locker room at the stadium."

Kennedy liked to let people think he didn't work out, but Nash said, "He actually worked out more than just about anybody. He wanted a mystique like it was all natural, that he didn't have to work at staying at a plump 300-whatever."

"His rookie year I thought he played as well as anybody could," Wyman said. "I was a rookie and had no clue. I was lost for a while, and he went right in there and really did well."

But Bosworth aggravated a previous shoulder injury in the playoff game, and by early in the next season he had been reduced to a one-armed tackler. He had surgery on his left shoulder on October 31, 1988, and finished the season with 82 tackles in 10 starts.

In the second game of 1989, he hurt his right shoulder while trying to make a one-armed tackle against the Phoenix Cardinals and was placed on injured reserve for the second straight year. Bosworth's well-known use of steroids was suspected to have caused the arthritic deterioration in his shoulders. He failed a physical in July 1990 and was cut—having started just 24 games over three seasons.

"He was a good linebacker," Nash said, "but because of injury he didn't end up fulfilling what he thought he could do."

He might not have done much on the field, but he sure cashed in off the field. He had been paid $3.75 million over his three seasons with the Seahawks, and he had an insurance policy that reportedly would guarantee the remaining $7.3 million.

Bosworth became a multimedia figure, with his controversial 1988 book, *The Boz: Confessions of a Modern Day Anti-Hero,* and his movies. When he was released by Seattle, he already was busy filming a movie called *The Brotherhood.* His most well-known film was the 1991 action flick, *Stone Cold,* and he was cast as the title character in a short-lived 1997 TV show called *Lawless.*

Wyman had to testify about Bosworth's injuries for the insurance claim, and Wyman laughed when he saw his former teammate on the stand.

"When I saw him crying in court, 'Oh, I'll never play again,' it was the best acting job he ever did," Wyman said. "I know it's true because I've seen some of his movies on HBO."

KRIEG'S DREAM DRIVE AND FREDDIE'S NIGHTMARE

After Dave Krieg had put together the drive of his life, the Seahawks offense should have gotten another chance.

Fredd Young appeared to have given them one with his interception of Warren Moon's pass in overtime. But the replay official didn't see it that way, and the Houston Oilers continued their march to the winning field goal and a 23–20 victory in the AFC wild-card game on January 3, 1988.

Moon dropped back to pass at the Houston 37, and his throw was batted by defensive end Jeff Bryant. Young dived and seemed to scoop the ball into his arms before it hit the ground. But head linesman Dale Hamer ruled it an incompletion, and replay official Tony Veteri said reviews of the play were inconclusive.

"We could not tell whether the ball hit or not, so we had to go with the call on the field," Veteri told pool reporter John McClain of the *Houston Chronicle.* "We did not get a clear view whether he caught the ball before it hit the ground. Part of his arm covered up the ball. So we had to go with the call on the field."

And with that, the Oilers drove 61 yards to set up Tony Zendejas for the deciding 42-yard field goal, sending Houston into a divisional playoff, where they were blown out 34–10 by the Denver Broncos.

If Young's interception had stood, the Seahawks would have had the ball at Houston's 40-yard line—and likely would have been the ones to make the winning kick. They felt they had given themselves that chance.

"I knew I had it," Young told reporters. "There wasn't anything I could do but catch the ball. There was no possible way that ball can hit the ground."

Coach Chuck Knox agreed: "Our observation showed it was an interception. But they ruled otherwise, and there's nothing we can do about it. The game is gone and lost. Nothing we can say or do is going to bring it back."

The Seahawks had brought themselves back in the final two minutes of regulation with one of the biggest touchdown drives in team history. After Zendejas had bounced a 29-yard kickoff the left upright with 1:47 left and Houston leading 20–13, Krieg drove the Seahawks 80 yards for the tying score. It took four tries to get the initial first down as Krieg hit Steve Largent for a 10-yard gain on fourth-and-10. Krieg later found Ray Butler for a 32-yard play on third-and-10 that got the Seahawks to the Houston 12, and the quarterback finished the clutch drive with a touchdown pass to Largent with 26 seconds left.

"It was a shame because that was Dave Krieg's defining moment," said safety Paul Moyer, who missed the game with an injury. "If we could have won that playoff, it would have catapulted Dave into that top tier of quarterbacks."

The Seahawks got the ball first in overtime, but they couldn't make anything out of their possession, and they couldn't get the call they needed to extend a season that had begun with Super Bowl aspirations. The Seahawks had made the playoffs for the third time in five years, but they once again had fallen short of expectations.

Defense had doomed them throughout the 9–6 strike season, including a 41–20 loss in the season finale in Kansas City that had sent them to the Astrodome rather than kept them home at the Kingdome for the game against the Oilers. The Seahawks played the wild-card game without Curt Warner, who had a sprained left ankle, and the Oilers used their three-headed backfield of

Mike Rozier, Alonzo Highsmith, and Allen Pinkett to accumulate 169 rushing yards and keep the ball away from Seattle. Houston owned the ball for 47:44, limiting Seattle's offense to just 20:21.

"We went into the game knowing we had to throw the ball, and we were concerned about our defense," Knox told reporters. "They moved the ball and were able to control it, and we struggled offensively and really couldn't keep our defense off the field as much as we would have liked to."

Despite all of that, the game hinged on one call that the replay official refused to overturn, and the Seahawks were left with no more do-overs in a 1987 season that fell short of expectations.

"That was terrible we lost that," Krieg said, "especially when you tie the game the way we did, with an 80-yard drive at the end."

Moyer, who watched the game on TV with Warner, said, "It was a very, very, very disappointing end to the season. We felt that was the most talented team we had."

EASLEY'S END

It was the messiest divorce between team and player in the history of the Seahawks, a tragic and ill-fitting end to the career of one of the best players ever to wear an NFL uniform, let alone a Seahawks jersey.

And it happened so quickly.

From the day he was drafted with the fourth pick in the 1981 draft, Kenny Easley was the Seahawks enforcer on defense and one of the best defenders in the NFL.

One of the hardest-hitting, most intimidating defenders in the league and a player who redefined the strong safety position, Easley went to five Pro Bowls from 1982 to 1986 and was voted to the All-Pro team from 1983 to 1985. For five years, he was the best safety in the NFL. He put the I-N-T in *intimidation*.

But in 1987 Easley didn't seem to run as fast or pack the same punch. He turned in a career-low 41 tackles, and in April 1988 the Seahawks chose to trade him to the Phoenix Cardinals

For five seasons in the early 1980s, Kenny Easley was the best safety in football. Photo courtesy of Getty Images.

for quarterback Kelly Stouffer. Some believe his role as union representative during the 1987 strike season played a part in the team's decision to trade him as well.

But the trade never went through because Easley's physical exam with the Cardinals revealed a previously undetected kidney disease. The team doctor reportedly was so concerned by the toxins in Easley's kidney that he called the paramedics. And then the Cardinals voided the trade (the Seahawks instead obtained Stouffer for draft picks).

Just like that, one of the NFL's shining defensive stars had winked out. Easley was forced to retire as he awaited a transplant.

Fellow safety Paul Moyer marveled at the fact that Easley somehow had played through the affliction in 1987.

"It was weird that this guy was playing in a season when most people would be bedridden," Moyer said. "He was playing pro football with almost complete kidney failure."

Easley blamed the degenerative kidney problem on pain medication he had taken during his playing days, and in April 1989 he sued the Seahawks and their trainer, doctors, and Advil supplier for failing to make him aware of the risks while continuing to feed him Advil so he could play. According to the lawsuit, Easley had been taking 20 pills a day to help with pain in his ankle. He developed the kidney problem in 1986, and by the time it was discovered in April 1988, he was in almost total kidney failure.

The lawsuit against the Seahawks and trainer Jim Whitesel was dropped in the fall of 1990, and Easley settled in 1991 with the team doctors and the New York lab that distributed the Advil to the Seahawks.

Easley underwent a kidney transplant in 1990, and he said he never heard a word from the organization that was then owned by Ken Behring and still coached by Chuck Knox. The Seahawks admittedly held a grudge against Easley for several years, and the former safety in turn maintained a distance from the team for more than a decade, rebuffing overtures to be inducted into the team's Ring of Honor. It wasn't until 2002 that he relented and allowed the team to honor him.

"It was the right time for my family and myself," he told reporters then. "This is a new organization. These people that run the team now had nothing to do with what transpired back in the early '80s, and it would be foolish not to take advantage of the generosity that these folks are extending to my family and myself. All of the stars lined up correctly, and it was time to do it."

His former teammates think it's time to put him in the Hall of Fame as well.

"Kenny Easley is the best player ever to play his position. Hands down. He's the finest safety," Moyer declared. "How is he not in the Hall of Fame? Everyone talks about Ronnie Lott, but if Kenny was a 100, Ronnie Lott was a 97. Ronnie didn't have Kenny's speed. Kenny could have been a quarterback, wide receiver, professional golfer, tennis player. He was a phenomenal athlete."

So good, in fact, that the Chicago Bulls picked him in the 10th round of the NBA draft when the three-time All-American safety came out of UCLA in 1981. But Easley stuck to the NFL and quickly established himself as one of the league's best defenders.

Quarterback Dave Krieg said Easley "might be the best athlete that I've ever seen play the game. He had the instincts and knowledge of the game. He returned punts, played corner, played safety."

In 1981 he was named AFC defensive rookie of the year. In 1983, when he intercepted seven passes, he was named AFC defensive player of the year. And in 1984, after he picked off 10 passes (tying John Harris's team record) and returned two for touchdowns, he was the NFL defensive player of the year. He later was named to the NFL's all-decade team for the 1980s.

"He was one of the best defensive backs in the 1980s," said nose tackle Joe Nash, who played with Easley for six seasons. "You look at highlights of him destroying people. He started that big strong safety that was a run stopper and could intimidate people."

Perhaps the best endorsement for Easley's Hall of Fame candidacy comes from former receiver Steve Largent, who is the only career Seahawk in the Hall of Fame.

"I think had his career not been ended by the kidney problem, he would be in the Hall of Fame right now," Largent said. "He was clearly a great player. I still think he should be in the Hall of Fame."

YOUNG WAS RESTLESS

It's hard to know what would have happened had the Seahawks paid to keep Fredd Young instead of trading him, but it's also hard to argue with what and whom the team got in return for the play-making linebacker.

In 1988 Young was coming off his fourth straight Pro Bowl—his second as a starting linebacker—and he felt slighted by the fact that the Seahawks were paying second-year linebacker Brian Bosworth more than him.

Young, the Seahawks' third-round pick in 1984, had signed a four-year contract in August 1987 and reportedly was due to make $350,000 in 1988 and $425,000 in 1989. Two days after he signed that deal, the Seahawks signed Bosworth to a 10-year contract worth $11 million. Young, who had been to the Pro Bowl in all three of his seasons (two on special teams), was not happy.

So Young held out. He missed training camp and the first game of the 1988 season, and he was ready to sit out the entire year, so on September 8 the Seahawks traded him to the Indianapolis Colts for two first-round draft picks.

Fellow linebacker Dave Wyman disagreed with Young's stance, but he agreed with Young's reasoning. "Fredd was probably a lot better player than Brian. He knew what Brian was all about, not worth $11 million," Wyman said.

In an effort to appease Young, Seahawks president Mike McCormack told reporters he had gone against policy and offered to upgrade Young's deal, boosting his 1990 salary to $800,000 and his 1991 salary to $900,000. But McCormack was not going to set precedent by tearing up the deal Young had just signed.

"You're always concerned about the messages you send out," McCormack said. "I think that was the biggest motivating force in saying that we would not renegotiate and tear up the contract that Fredd had with us."

McCormack also was dead set on getting two first-round picks or players of like ability. He explained, "I think if a player feels he can hold out and get traded to a team where he wants to go or just any place, we've established a pretty high price."

The Colts, who were among eight teams pursuing Young, paid the price both in picks and pennies. In addition to handing over their first-round choices in 1989 and 1990, they gave Young a five-year contract worth $4.5 million.

Unfortunately, Young, who had been allowed to freelance in Tom Catlin's Seattle defense, never fit into the Colts' defensive scheme. After recording 15 sacks in his two seasons as a starting linebacker for the Seahawks, Young recorded just two quarterback kills in three seasons with the Colts. And then he was out of football.

The Seahawks, meanwhile, made good use of the two first-round picks. In 1989 they drafted tackle Andy Heck, who went on to start 70 games at three line positions in five seasons in Seattle. The big hit was in 1990, when the Seahawks parlayed their two first-round picks into the third overall choice and obtained defensive tackle Cortez Kennedy.

Two seasons later, when Young was already out of football, Kennedy was named the NFL's defensive player of the year. He ended up going to eight Pro Bowls in an 11-year career that might eventually find him in the Hall of Fame.

THE CLUTCH

THE FIRST WIN

The 1976 Expansion Bowl that pitted the first-year units from Seattle and Tampa Bay was as ugly as any game the Seahawks have ever played. It was a game befitting two 0–5 teams that didn't know how to win—a game so bad that the teams set an unofficial record for ugliest contest while establishing true NFL records for penalties and yards lost to penalties.

The only good thing about the game is that the 43,812 fans who actually showed up to watch at the Big Sombrero in Tampa were spared the grisly scene of overtime. Of course, it figured that the guy who saved everyone from that fate would be an old-school linebacker who had won many games in a long NFL career before being relegated to the expansion Seahawks—and who probably was too tired to play an extra quarter.

Thus, Mike Curtis finished off the Seahawks' first victory by blocking Tampa Bay kicker Dave Green's 35-yard field-goal attempt with 42 seconds left, preserving Seattle's 13–10 lead and removing the goose egg from the Seahawks' win column.

Fittingly, the Bucs drew their 20th penalty on that play. It was an ugly end to a horribly played game in which the teams combined to set modern NFL records with 35 penalties and 310 penalty yards. The only game that was more penalized was a 1951 contest between Cleveland and Chicago, who combined for 37 flags for 374 yards.

THE SEAHAWKS' GAME-WINNING KICKS

(In overtime or with a minute or less remaining in regulation)

Before 2000

- **October 8, 1978:** Efren Herrera kicked a 19-yard field goal to beat Minnesota 29–28 on the final play.
- **November 26, 1978:** Herrera's 46-yarder with three seconds left gave Seattle a sweep of the Oakland Raiders—the first time since 1965 the Raiders had lost to the same team twice in one season.
- **November 27, 1983:** Norm Johnson's 42-yard kick 1:46 into overtime finished off the wildest game in Seahawks history, a 51–48 win over Kansas City.
- **November 13, 1988:** Johnson kicked the winning 46-yard field goal with a second left as Seattle topped Houston 27–24.
- **November 25, 1990:** Johnson hit from 40 yards three minutes into overtime, giving Seattle a 13–10 win over San Diego.
- **December 2, 1990:** A week after he beat the Chargers in overtime, Johnson repeated the feat against Houston, kicking a 42-yarder in a 13–10 overtime win.
- **November 30, 1992:** John Kasay converted a 32-yard field goal about 11 minutes into overtime to give Seattle its second win of the season, 16–13 over Denver.
- **October 24, 1993:** Seattle beat New England 10–9 after Kasay's extra point followed Brian Blades's one-yard touchdown catch from Rick Mirer with 25 seconds left.
- **November 20, 1994:** Kasay kicked the winning extra point after Mack Strong's seven-yard touchdown run with 42 seconds left, giving Seattle a 22–21 win over Tampa Bay.
- **November 29, 1998:** Todd Peterson hit a 48-yard field goal with one second left in a 20–18 victory against the Tennessee Oilers.

How ugly was the 1976 Expansion Bowl? Neither team was able to move the ball. Jim Zorn completed just 11 of 27 passes and Sherman Smith led the Seahawks with a mere 45 yards rushing. The Seahawks scored all 13 points in the second quarter, on a 15-yard pass from Zorn to Sam McCullum and two field goals by John Leypoldt. The Bucs did even worse under quarterback Steve Spurrier, who everyone later would learn was much better suited to be a college football coach.

As for Curtis, the heroic play in the final minute was his shining moment as a Seahawk. A first-round draft pick by the Baltimore Colts in 1965, Curtis had played in two Super Bowls, including the Colts' win over Dallas in Super Bowl V after the 1970 season. A four-time Pro Bowl player, he was the Colts' most valuable player in 1974 but was let go at age 32 after an injury-plagued 1975 season.

The Seahawks had happily scooped him up in the veteran allocation draft, where he was one of their biggest finds. Nicknamed "Mad Dog" and "Animal" elsewhere and "Face" in Seattle because of all of his battle scars, Curtis was just the kind of nasty leader coach Jack Patera wanted for his defense. He was the prototypical tough guy—so rough and tumble that, in a game against the Miami Dolphins in 1971, he had knocked out a fan who had run onto the field.

But Curtis apparently wasn't keen on trying to help a building team in the twilight of his career. After he finished as Seattle's second-leading tackler in 1976, he quickly found employment elsewhere. But he had made his mark with a clutch play that not only gave the Seahawks their first win, it also prevented Tampa Bay from winning the one game it might have had a chance to win in its first season.

Recalled receiver Steve Largent: "It wasn't a great game.... It was very fulfilling for us to finally win a game. We were playing the other bottomfeeders, the other first-year franchise. We were glad we didn't lose the game."

The Bucs, meanwhile, went on to lose all 14 games in 1976 and their first 12 in 1977—a 26-game losing streak that stands as the NFL record. The Bucs had been shut out three times in the first five games of 1976, and coach John McKay already had become frustrated as his team prepared to play the Seahawks. After a 21–0 loss to Cincinnati the week before, McKay uttered an instant classic response when asked what he thought of his team's execution: "I'm all for it."

KRIEG AND SKANSI RUIN DERRICK'S DAY

Derrick Thomas was on a mission. And for nearly 60 minutes, it looked like he had accomplished it. But then Dave Krieg and Paul Skansi ruined Thomas's historic day by making one of the biggest plays in Seahawks history.

Always one of the loudest stadiums in the NFL, Arrowhead in Kansas City was especially cranked up on November 11, 1990. It was Veterans Day, and the fans were helping Thomas, their star pass rusher, pay tribute to his father, a pilot who had been killed in action in Vietnam 18 years earlier. Thomas, already a star in just his second NFL season, had dedicated the game to his father, and a squadron of military jets had flown overhead before the game in tribute to the late air force captain.

Krieg recalled the scene vividly: "The crowd was really loud. The planes flew over. Derrick was fired up. The crowd was real wild."

It only got wilder once the game started, as Thomas proceeded to put on one of the greatest individual performances in NFL history. He spent the entire game in the Seahawks backfield, setting an NFL record by sacking Krieg seven times. But the one he missed is the one everyone remembers most, because Krieg shook off the eighth sack and fired a 25-yard pass to Skansi in the end zone to tie the score with no time left, and Norm Johnson's extra point gave the Seahawks an improbable 17–16 victory and ended a decade of disaster in Kansas City.

The Seahawks had not won in Kansas City in eight visits over the previous 10 years, and it looked like the Chiefs would stretch the Seahawks' losing skid to nine as Thomas and a stellar Kansas City defense shut down Krieg and company all day.

"Every time Dave went back to pass, [Thomas] was around him," defensive tackle Joe Nash remembered.

"We were taking a beating on offense," Krieg said. "Fortunately our defense was doing a good job."

Indeed, despite the dominance of Thomas and the Chiefs defense, the Seahawks had hung tough and trailed just 16–10—the Chiefs' touchdown coming when Thomas sacked Krieg in the end zone and Dan Saleaumua recovered the fumble—when they got the ball back with 48 seconds to play.

Krieg found fullback John L. Williams on a 16-yard pass and then hit Tommy Kane for 25, putting Seattle at Kansas City's 25-yard line with four seconds left, just enough time for one play. As Krieg dropped back to throw, Thomas again met him in the backfield, as he had done nearly all day. Thomas had his arms around Krieg, but Krieg whirled away, stepped to the side, and fired a pass to Skansi in the middle of the end zone.

Linebacker David Wyman attributed it all to Krieg's competitiveness: "Derrick Thomas missed his eighth sack because Dave—5'11" and 190 pounds sopping wet—makes him whiff. It was so improbable because Dave physically vs. Derrick Thomas, there's no way. But I swear Dave willed that to happen."

Despite getting sacked seven times by Kansas City's Derrick Thomas, Dave Krieg had the last laugh when he threw the game-winning touchdown in this emotionally charged 1990 game. Photo courtesy of Getty Images.

THE SEAHAWKS' GAME-WINNING KICKS

(In overtime or with a minute or less remaining in regulation)
2000 and After

- **November 5, 2000:** Rian Lindell nailed a 48-yard kick in driving wind and rain as time expired, giving Seattle a 17–15 win against San Diego.
- **September 9, 2001:** Lindell's 52-yard kick with three seconds left gave Seattle a 9–6 win over Cleveland in the season opener.
- **December 2, 2001:** After missing a 48-yarder to win with seven seconds left in regulation, Lindell's 24-yard kick on the first series of overtime gave the Hawks a 13–10 win over San Diego.
- **December 30, 2001:** Lindell blasted a 54-yard kick with no time left to beat San Diego 25–22, his third game-winning kick against the Chargers in two years and second of the month.
- **October 27, 2002:** After missing three previous kicks, Lindell booted a 20-yard field goal with 25 seconds left to lift Seattle to a 17–14 win over Dallas.
- **December 29, 2002:** Lindell's 24-yard field goal on Seattle's second overtime possession gave his team a 31–28 victory over San Diego—Lindell's fourth winning kick against the Chargers in three years.
- **September 21, 2003:** Josh Brown kicked the extra point after Matt Hasselbeck threw a 3-yard touchdown pass to Koren Robinson with a minute left, and Seattle rallied to beat St. Louis 24–23.
- **October 23, 2005:** After Jordan Babineaux intercepted Drew Bledsoe's pass, Brown hit a 50-yard field goal on the final play to beat Dallas 13–10.
- **November 27, 2005:** After Jay Feely missed three potential winning kicks for the Giants, Brown's 36-yarder in overtime gave Seattle a 24–21 win.
- **September 10, 2006:** Brown accounted for all of Seattle's points in a 9–6 win in Detroit, hitting from 51 yards as time expired in the first half and winning the game on the final play with a 42-yard kick.

- **October 15, 2006:** Brown's 54-yard field goal to give the Hawks a 30–28 win in St. Louis was the third-longest final-play kick in NFL history until two other NFL kickers nailed game-winners from 60 yards or more in the 2006 season.
- **November 12, 2006:** Brown completed a personal season sweep of the Rams with a 38-yard field goal with nine seconds left that gave Seattle a 24–22 win.
- **December 3, 2006:** Brown beat the Broncos 23–20 in Denver on a 50-yard kick with five seconds left. It was his sixth game-winner in two seasons, and he tied Lindell for the most game-winning kicks in franchise history.

So instead of enjoying the historic seven-sack performance on a day he had dedicated to his father, Thomas was left to rue the one that got away. "That last sack I didn't get is the one I'm going to remember," he told reporters afterward.

Krieg, meanwhile, was happy the official had not ruled him down. "I'm glad the referee didn't call in the grasp because that would have been a heck of a way to end that game. [Thomas] had his hands on my hips. I just managed to shake him away from me, fortunately."

Skansi was one of four wide receivers running "go" routes on the play, and he faced the task of getting open against one of the best safeties in the NFL, Deron Cherry. Skansi told reporters after the game that it was probably fortuitous that Thomas had forced Krieg to buy time.

"If he'd thrown it on time, they might have converged on it," Skansi said. "I was still five yards out of the end zone when he started to scramble."

Krieg said he did not see Skansi catch the ball in front of Cherry, but he knew he had because he didn't hear a sound. "It is the quietest I've ever heard Arrowhead."

And it certainly was the loudest the visitors' locker room had been in a decade of use by the Seahawks.

"We just went crazy after that game," Krieg said. "It was a whole team effort. Everybody felt a part of it."

As the Seahawks waited at the airport to fly back to Seattle, players began to fill a little lounge, and coach Chuck Knox had the bartender set them up. "Chuck took out his credit card and bought drinks for everyone, emptied out the bar," Krieg chuckled.

Wyman remembers it just as clearly: "The whole team jammed into that small bar, celebrating. And Chuck was into it, because it was such a relief and the way we won."

It was certainly a day worth celebrating, as the Seahawks ended a decade of futility in Kansas City with a win that Krieg says was nearly as exciting as when they upset the heavily favored Dolphins in Miami in the divisional playoffs in 1983.

"It brings chills up my spine just remembering it right now," said Krieg.

Little did he know at the time, but that would be Krieg's final game as a Seahawk in Kansas City. He missed the 1991 contest because of an injury. But it wasn't his last game in Kansas City; he signed with the Chiefs in 1992 when the Seahawks decided they no longer wanted him.

WIN AND THEY'RE IN

The Seahawks have made a habit out of squeezing into the playoffs in the final week of the season. It's how they got in the first time, when they shocked the league by making a run all the way to the AFC title game. It's also how they won their first division title in 1988, how they made the playoffs in 2003, and how they won the division in 2004.

In all, six of their playoff appearances have been determined in the final week or two of the season. Their 1983 season is documented elsewhere in this book, but following are the other late-season, playoff-clinching victories in the history of the franchise.

Escape from L.A.

The Seahawks entered the final game of 1988 needing a win over the Raiders in Los Angeles to claim their first AFC West division title and the accompanying playoff berth and bye. The Seahawks

SEAHAWKS' TOP KICKERS FROM 50 YARDS

Kicker	Pct.	Seasons
John Kasay	.600 (6 of 10)	1991–94
Josh Brown	.588 (10 of 17)	2003–06
Rian Lindell	.583 (7 of 12)	2000–02
Todd Peterson	.429 (3 of 7)	1995–99
Norm Johnson	.385 (10 of 26)	1982–90

Longest Final-Play Field Goals in NFL History

Yards	Kicker (Team)	Opponent	Date
63	Tom Dempsey (NO)	Detroit	11/8/1970
62	Matt Bryant (TB)	Philadelphia	10/22/2006
60	Rob Bironas (Tenn)	Indianapolis	12/2/2006
56	Paul Edinger (Minn)	Green Bay	10/23/2005
54	Doug Pelfrey (Cin)	Philadelphia	12/24/1994
54	Pete Stoyanovich (KC)	Denver	11/16/1997
54	Rian Lindell (Sea)	San Diego	12/30/2001
54	Josh Brown (Sea)	St. Louis	10/15/2006

were sitting at 8–7 and had no chance at a wild-card spot because Cleveland and Houston would end up with 10 wins each and face each other in the wild-card game.

The Seahawks already had beaten the Raiders in a 35–27 shootout in a Monday night game three weeks earlier, so it figured that this one would feature plenty of offense, too.

Dave Krieg, who had thrown five touchdown passes in the first meeting, threw for 410 yards and four touchdowns in this one, and John L. Williams had 180 yards receiving for Seattle, including a 75-yard screen play for a touchdown, as the Seahawks won 43–37.

"Our offense played pretty darn good that game," Krieg said. "I wished we would have done that in 1983 against those guys."

The game was not over until the Raiders' Hail Mary pass on the final play fell incomplete. Paul Moyer made sure Willie Gault, the

Raiders' high-jumping deep threat, could not get to the ball by grabbing Gault's pants and stepping on his foot so he couldn't jump.

"It was a huge monkey off our back," Moyer said of the win. "We never had won the West and never had a bye going into the playoffs."

Roll Reversal

In 1999 Mike Holmgren's first Seahawks squad got off to a surprising 8–2 start and was seemingly a lock to make the postseason. But then the Hawks lost four games in a row, and they suddenly needed to win their final two games or get a lot of help. They ended up with a little of both.

Coming off a wild overtime loss to the Denver Broncos, the Seahawks hosted the Kansas City Chiefs in the penultimate game of the season and the final regular-season game ever at the Kingdome. The Chiefs had been going the opposite direction of the Seahawks, with four straight wins since Seattle's 31–19 victory in the first meeting that season. The Chiefs merely needed to beat Seattle to win the AFC West. But Elvis Grbac threw three interceptions, Jon Kitna threw two touchdown passes, and the Seahawks won 23–14 to secure their first winning season since 1990.

All Seattle needed after that was a win in the season finale against the New York Jets at the Meadowlands. But they didn't get it. They lost 19–9 in Bill Parcells's final game as coach of the Jets. Fortunately for the Seahawks, the Oakland Raiders beat the Chiefs, and the Seahawks won the AFC West courtesy of their season sweep of Kansas City.

Jets running back Curtis Martin couldn't believe his ears when informed the Seahawks had made the postseason. "What? We beat them and they're still in the playoffs?"

They weren't for long, losing to Miami 20–17 in a wild-card game at the Kingdome the following week.

Road Worriers

The 2003 Seahawks had lost six straight road games as they went to San Francisco for a playoffs-or-bust finale against the 49ers. They rallied from a 14–0 deficit in the first quarter to win 24–17

Despite a spate of injuries to the defending NFC champs, the 9–7 Hawks were only a field goal away from returning to the NFC Championship game.

behind two touchdown passes from Matt Hasselbeck and a scoring run by Shaun Alexander. Then the Seahawks had to sit back and watch.

Because they had played their final game on Saturday, they had to wait to see how teams fared Sunday before they knew whether they had made the playoffs and, if they had, where they would play in the wild-card round.

After the Seahawks' victory, Coach Holmgren told reporters that he had jokingly encouraged his players "if they don't go to church, I want them in church tomorrow, and see if one of these teams can help us a little bit."

The Seahawks got the required help and ended up going back to Green Bay for what turned out to be a memorable overtime loss.

How the NFC West Was Won

At the end of the 2004 season, the Seahawks were angling for their first NFC West division title and the home playoff game that would accompany it. The only obstacles were the Atlanta Falcons, who planned to rest starting quarterback Michael Vick after a short appearance in the regular-season finale. No problem, right?

Well, the Seahawks didn't get the division title until the play *after* the clock had reached double zeroes. That's because they had to stop Warrick Dunn on a two-point conversion after the Falcons had scored on the final play of regulation. The tackle by Chad Brown and Rocky Bernard enabled Seattle to escape with a 28–26 win and the right to host the division rival St. Louis Rams in a wild-card game the next week.

Even without starting receiver Koren Robinson, who was benched for the game after missing a team walk-through the previous day, Hasselbeck threw for two scores and ran for a third. But the Seahawks gave up 204 yards rushing to the NFC South champion Falcons, who sat Vick after he had led them to a 10–7 lead in the first three series. After the game, Holmgren said he thanked Vick for sitting out the second half.

Of course, the home playoff game did little to help the Seahawks, who lost to the Rams for the third time that season.

Eight Is Enough, but Nine Is Better

The 2006 Seahawks battled injuries as much as their opponents all season, but they still managed to become the first team in six years to reach the playoffs the season after losing in the Super Bowl. They were just lucky they were playing in one of the league's two worst divisions.

The Seahawks started 8–4 despite losing Hasselbeck and Alexander to injuries for large parts of the season and despite never starting the entire number one offense. But they lost three straight games—and still won the NFC West for the third straight year because none of the other teams could finish better than 8–8.

Mike Holmgren was in no mood to apologize for backing into the division title. "Our first goal was to win the division, and we won the division," he told reporters. "People can say whatever they want about that—and frankly, I don't care...I'll take it."

The Seahawks did manage to avoid the ignominy of becoming just the second NFL team to win a division with an 8–8 record when they won in Tampa Bay to close the season. And they missed a second straight appearance in the NFC title game by three points when they lost an overtime playoff game in Chicago.

IT AIN'T OVER TILL IT'S OVER

UPSET IN MIAMI

The Seahawks weren't even given a chance.

After all, they were just a 9–7 wild-card team with a shaky defense, a first-year coach, and an undrafted quarterback. And they were going against the Miami Dolphins, the defending AFC champions coached by Don Shula and quarterbacked by star rookie Dan Marino.

Just about everyone thought Chuck Knox's Hawks had no shot at beating the Dolphins at the Orange Bowl. But the Seahawks had surprised people all season, and they knew they had another left in them after they had dominated Denver 31–7 in a wild-card game the previous week.

"We went down there as heavy underdogs," wide receiver Steve Largent said. "I remember going out on the field, everybody on our team felt really positive about our chances of winning the game."

Paul Moyer, a rookie safety that season, said Knox pumped them full of confidence.

"When Chuck spoke, we believed him," Moyer said. "He said this was the most talented team he had ever had. Reggie McKenzie said the same thing. So did Charle Young. Guys who had played on playoff teams. Chuck really sold us that we had a great game plan, that we were going to go out and win this game. The rest of the team followed along."

And when it came down to it, the team followed Largent, Dave Krieg, and Curt Warner to victory. They combined to put the Seahawks ahead and special teams sealed the deal as Seattle scored 10 points in the final two minutes to upset the heavily favored Dolphins 27–20 in the divisional playoff game on December 31, 1983. It was the Seahawks' second straight playoff victory in a magical ride through the 1983 season that ended the next week with a loss to the Los Angeles Raiders in the AFC title game.

After the Dolphins had taken a 20–17 lead with 3:43 to play, the Seahawks took over at their own 34-yard line. Two runs set up a third-and-two, and Krieg found Largent for the first time all game, on a 16-yard pass over the middle.

Seattle wideout Steve Largent gets past the outstretched arm of Miami's Glenn Blackwood in the Seahawks' stunning 27–20 upset in the 1983 Divisional Playoff game at the Orange Bowl in Miami. Photo courtesy of Focus on Sports/Getty Images.

"The next play was a post corner route," Largent said. "I was double-covered and got the guy to bite on the post."

It ended in a 40-yard gain that set up Warner's two-yard touchdown run, which put Seattle up 24–20 with 1:48 left.

Then the Seattle special teams answered a challenge from coach Rusty Tillman to come up with a big play against Fulton Walker, the Dolphins' talented return specialist who had averaged 26.7 yards per kick return during the 1983 season and had also scored on a kick return in the previous season's Super Bowl against Washington. Mark Hicks answered Tillman's call, stripping the ball from Walker so Sam Merriman could recover. That set up Norm Johnson's 37-yard field goal 24 seconds later.

The Dolphins still had 1:15 left to try to tie the score, but Walker fumbled the next kickoff as well, and Dan Doornink recovered for the Seahawks, who carried coach Chuck Knox off the field as they celebrated the biggest win in franchise history.

"I still think it was the most celebrated moment that I had as a Seahawk because we were heavy underdogs playing on their field," Largent said of a win that is considered one of the biggest upsets in NFL playoff history.

The Seahawks stayed with the Dolphins the whole way. Marino threw two touchdown passes in the first half, a 19-yarder to Dan Johnson and a 32-yarder to Mark Duper. After the first one, Zachary Dixon put Seattle in good position with a 59-yard kick return, and Krieg finished a six-play, 38-yard drive with a six-yard scoring pass to Cullen Bryant.

The Seahawks finally got the lead in the third quarter after John Harris recovered a fumble and Warner capped a 55-yard drive with a one-yard touchdown run. The defense got the ball back again, on Kerry Justin's interception, and Johnson put Seattle ahead 17–13 early in the fourth quarter.

The Seattle defense stopped Miami with 4:44 left, and it looked like Warner, who finished with 113 yards on 29 carries, would take over and finish the upset. But Ground Chuck outfoxed himself with a pass play, and when Largent ran a different route than Krieg was expecting, Gerald Small intercepted the ball and returned it to the Seattle 16-yard line. Three plays later,

BLOCK PARTY

Joe Nash holds the team record of 10 blocked kicks (eight on field goals). Asked the secret to his success over his club-record 218 games, he said, "Getting skinny."

"Most of it was Jake [Green] and Jeff [Bryant]," he said. "They both knew how to rush the kick. [Blockers] couldn't just zone in on me because Jake or Jeff would get by. With me, it was a matter of turning sideways, stepping over interlocked legs. I probably got through 50 percent of the time. It was being able to get far enough back to get your hands on it. If my reach was six inches longer, I probably would have blocked 10 more."

Woody Bennett ran in from the 2-yard line to put the Dolphins ahead again, 20–17.

But that was the last chance Marino and Miami would get, as the Seahawks went on to upset Shula's defending AFC champions in what Largent called "one of the best games the Seahawks ever played."

TWO GAMES, ONE LOSS

It looked like they had done it. After two years of playing second and third fiddle in the remade NFC West, it looked like the Seahawks finally had played their way into the top chair.

In October 2004 a Qwest Field–record crowd of 66,940 had come to watch the Seahawks overtake the St. Louis Rams as the best in the West. And for three and a half quarters, the Seahawks seemed to have done just that, taking a 27–10 lead against the defending division champs. But their lead melted in the final six minutes of regulation, and the Rams finished off the improbable comeback with a quick strike in overtime to beat Seattle 33–27 and prevent the Seahawks from starting a season 4–0 for the first time in franchise history.

Seattle wide receiver Koren Robinson said it felt like his team had lost two games. It sure seemed like they played two. The

Seahawks had imposed their will on the Rams in the first half, taking a 24–7 lead thanks to huge advantages in first downs (17–5) and yards (306–122). Ken Lucas had intercepted two of Marc Bulger's passes, Matt Hasselbeck had thrown two touchdown passes, and Shaun Alexander had rushed for 98 yards and a touchdown.

"We had this game won," Alexander said afterward, summing up the Seahawks' attitude from halftime until the Rams' barrage was over.

It was a case of complacency, as the Seahawks offense got conservative, and the defense, which had entered the game as the top-ranked unit in the NFL, got burned. In the third quarter the Seahawks offense was on the field for a mere seven plays and earned just one first down, largely because of Coach Holmgren's conservative play calling.

"We let the defense down in the second half," Alexander said of an offense that gained a mere 86 yards and three first downs in the third and fourth quarters. "They had to play almost the entire game because we didn't do anything."

In the fourth quarter the Rams did it all. First, Bulger hit tight end Brandon Manumaleuna with an eight-yard scoring pass. Then, after the Rams stuffed Alexander on third-and-one, Shaun McDonald returned a punt 39 yards and Bulger hit Kevin Curtis on a 41-yard scoring pass on the next play. The Seahawks failed to get a first down on their next series as well and gave the ball back to the Rams at their own 36-yard line with 1:25 left. Bulger hit Isaac Bruce for a 27-yard pass, and his 16-yard throw to Dane Looker set the Rams up for Jeff Wilkins's tying 36-yard field goal. It all happened in five minutes and 34 seconds.

"They made big plays that didn't consume too much of the clock. And, really, that was the story," Holmgren said.

The Rams continued to move the ball through the air in overtime. Bulger found Torry Holt for a 13-yard gain on third-and-six, and then the quarterback burned the Seahawks on a third-down blitz by hitting a streaking McDonald for the winning 52-yard score.

"We played like crap at every position on defense," said defensive end Grant Wistrom, who then was in his first season with the

Matt Hasselbeck helped lead the Hawks to a 24–7 lead over Western rival St. Louis with a pair of first-half touchdowns on October 10, 2004, but the wheels came off and the Rams prevailed, ultimately knocking Seattle out of the playoffs that season.

Seahawks after spending his first six with the Rams. "That's what the problem was—just total breakdown. We weren't getting pressure on [Bulger], and guys were running around free because he had so much time to throw. We pretty much self-destructed out there."

Center Robbie Tobeck likened the collapse to a boxing match: "You got a guy on the ropes, you've got to finish him. You can't let a good team like that off the ropes, and we did."

The devastating defeat sent the Seahawks on a three-game losing streak and was the first of three losses that season to the Rams, who swept the season series and then knocked the Hawks out of the playoffs by winning at Qwest Field again.

ONE FOR THE BIRDS

In 2003 Mike Holmgren's new-look Seahawks were still a work in progress, not yet the perennial playoff team they would soon become, let alone a Super Bowl contender. When they went to Baltimore that season, they took a 7–3 record built largely against weaker opponents. So the game against the Ravens and their stout defense was a chance for the Seahawks to prove their abilities once and for all.

Matt Hasselbeck certainly proved his, throwing five touchdown passes as the Seahawks stormed to a 17-point lead against the league's third-ranked defense. But then the fourth quarter arrived, and the Seahawks melted under the pressure of their own heightened expectations as the Ravens rallied for a 44–41 overtime victory.

"I thought we were making a statement. I really did," Hasselbeck told reporters after the game. "I felt this was it. Then something happened."

Yeah, Seattle's special teams and secondary self-destructed. First, Baltimore safety Ed Reed blocked Tom Rouen's punt and ran it back 16 yards for a touchdown that cut the lead to 41–31. And then the Seahawks suddenly could not stop Anthony Wright and the Ravens' pedestrian offense. It didn't hurt that the Ravens got a little lucky with some help from the officials.

After the blocked field goal, the Ravens got the ball back and marched 71 yards in about three minutes. The Ravens got a lucky bounce during the drive when Wright's pass on fourth-and-28 went off the hands of Marcus Robinson and into the arms of Frank Sanders for a 44-yard gain. Wright, who had begun the season as the Ravens' number three quarterback, finished the drive with a 9-yard scoring pass to Robinson—their fourth touchdown hookup of the game.

The Seahawks recovered the onside kick, but Hasselbeck couldn't convert a fourth-and-one sneak, and the Ravens took over with 39 seconds left. A 44-yard pass-interference penalty against rookie cornerback Marcus Trufant set the Ravens up for Matt Stover's 40-yard field goal with no time left.

BIG RETURNS

The 1998 defense was perhaps the best bunch of ballhawks the Seahawks have ever assembled. They set the NFL record with 13 touchdowns on returns—10 on defense and three on special teams. The Seahawks scored on eight interceptions, the second-highest figure in NFL history and one more than the 1984 Seattle defense scored. Joey Galloway took back two punts for touchdowns, Steve Broussard ran back a kickoff, and Shawn Springs and Darrin Smith each returned two interceptions.

The Seahawks intercepted seven passes against San Diego in December 1998, the second-most interceptions in a game in NFL history. That was one better than the 1984 defense tallied in a 45–0 shutout of Kansas City.

Wright then drove the Ravens 55 yards in overtime, once again connecting with Robinson on a huge play—a 19-yard completion on third-and-15—to set up Stover's winning 42-yard kick.

The Seahawks knew they had made far too many mistakes to have deserved the win, but they also knew the officials had made a huge mistake of their own. The NFL admitted the error the next day.

On their drive to the tying field goal, the Ravens should have begun with far less than the 39 seconds they had when they got the ball. On the Seahawks' final possession, they were wrongly flagged for an ineligible receiver on second down. The penalty stopped the clock with 1:03 left, and referee Tom White failed to restart the game clock. If he had, the Seahawks could have run the clock down to about 12 seconds by the time the Ravens received the ball again. That would have been time enough for only one or two plays.

"That's how I was thinking," Holmgren told reporters that day. "Then, all of a sudden, the whole thing changed."

Mike Peireira, the NFL's supervisor of officials, acknowledged the error the next day.

"That was unfortunate," Holmgren said of the mistake. "But you know what? There were many, *many* times in that football game where if we make a play the game's over. I appreciate the league being very candid about it. Nothing changes. But we had chances, boy, as a team. It had nothing to do with the officials. We had our chances, and we just didn't do it when we needed to do it."

MONDAY NIGHT MELTDOWN

The Seahawks had to be thinking: didn't we already live this nightmare? They had already blown one game they had in hand during the 2004 season, losing to the St. Louis Rams despite leading by 17 points in the fourth quarter.

Two months later, a similar game played out as the Seahawks hosted the Dallas Cowboys on *Monday Night Football*. The Cowboys rallied with 14 points in the final 1:45 and knocked off the Seahawks 43–39 in one of the highest-scoring games in Seattle history.

It started with a questionable touchdown pass from Vinny Testaverde to Keyshawn Johnson, who appeared to get just one foot in bounds in the back of the end zone. The 34-yard score came with 1:45 to play, and officials erroneously eschewed a video review, so the Cowboys trailed just 39–36.

They then put themselves in position to go ahead when Jason Witten recovered Billy Cundiff's onside kick at the Dallas 43-yard line. On the eighth play of the drive, Julius Jones capped a 198-yard rushing day when he ran 17 yards through a gaping hole in the defense for the go-ahead touchdown with 32 seconds left.

It was the end of a roller-coaster Monday night game in which the Seahawks first led 14–3, then allowed Dallas to score 26 unanswered points in the second and third quarters, including two touchdown runs by Jones. Seattle then scored 25 points in the next 25 minutes, with two touchdown runs by Shaun Alexander and a touchdown pass from Matt Hasselbeck, who threw for 414 yards and three scores. Seattle's last score came on a 32-yard run by Alexander with 2:46 remaining.

The Cowboys then drove 64 yards in 1:01, ending with Testaverde's dubious scoring pass to Johnson. Two days later the

Seahawks fans express their displeasure after the team lost to the Dallas Cowboys on *Monday Night Football* in December 2004 in Seattle. Dallas erased a 10-point deficit with less than two minutes to play in a stunning 43–39 comeback win.

NFL admitted the play should have been reviewed, and Coach Holmgren stated emphatically that his review of the game tape showed it was not a touchdown because Johnson had indeed gotten only one foot in bounds.

DID YOU KNOW...

The Seahawks' biggest comeback was from a 20–0 second-quarter deficit in Denver in 1995. The Seahawks won 31–27.

After his team dropped to 6–6, Holmgren was concerned the blown leads against St. Louis and Dallas might end up costing the Seahawks a playoff spot. They didn't, because the Seahawks won three of their final four and won the weak NFC West with a 9–7 record.

Of course, it could have—and should have—been an 11–5 record, which would have given the Seahawks a first-round bye. Instead, they hosted the Rams the next week and fell to their division rivals for the third time that season—Seattle's second straight one-and-done playoff experience.

EXTRA! EXTRA! READ ALL ABOUT IT!

K.C. MASTERPIECE

The Seahawks never would have made it to the 1983 AFC Championship game, let alone the playoffs, if they hadn't come out on top in the highest-scoring game since the NFL merger.

Sputtering along with a 6–6 record that season, Seattle desperately needed a win against the Kansas City Chiefs to stay alive in the playoff hunt. Little did the Seahawks know what it would take to get the victory.

It would take Curt Warner's club-record 207 yards and three touchdowns. It would take two clutch field goals by Norm Johnson. It would take four rallies from deficits. It would take big plays from Dave Krieg and Zachary Dixon. And, finally, it would take a lot of points to beat the Chiefs 51–48 in what became the highest-scoring game since the NFL and AFL merged in 1970. The 99-point, post-merger record stood until 2004, when Cleveland and Cincinnati tallied a 106-point shootout.

The Seahawks and Chiefs combined for 13 touchdowns, 962 yards in offense, and 59 first downs. Even after all that, the Seahawks needed Johnson's 42-yard field goal with two seconds left to send the game into overtime and another 42-yarder shortly thereafter to win.

The Seahawks had to overcome six touchdowns (four passing, two rushing) by Kansas City quarterback Bill Kenney and three

ALEXANDER THE GREAT

Shaun Alexander is trying to make a case to join Steve Largent in the Pro Football Hall of Fame. In his first seven seasons, Alexander has achieved the following:

- He's one of two players in NFL history to score at least 15 touchdowns in five consecutive seasons.
- He's one of five players in NFL history to score at least 20 touchdowns in consecutive seasons.
- He's one of five players in NFL history to rush for back-to-back 1,600-yard seasons.
- He's the Seahawks' career leading rusher, with 8,713 yards.
- He holds the NFL record for most consecutive games of 100 or more yards rushing versus division foes (nine).
- He's one of four players in NFL history with two touchdown runs of 88 yards or more.
- Through 2006 he had recorded at least one run of 10 or more yards in 64 consecutive games, topping the record of 60 previously held by Barry Sanders (1995–98).
- He was named to three consecutive Pro Bowls (2003–05) and in 2005 became the first Seahawk to be named the NFL's most valuable player.

turnovers by Krieg, who atoned partially by catching an 11-yard pass from Steve Largent on one of the Seahawks' touchdown drives.

"That was the most amazing, unbelievable game," Krieg said. "We called a play on fourth down—I don't know what they were thinking, they must have run out of plays or something—Steve throws it to me.... I'd like to see it again how I did that."

Kenney staked the Chiefs to a 28–14 halftime lead, but the Seahawks rallied to take a 31–28 lead thanks largely to two fumbles by the Chiefs in the third quarter. Kenney's one-yard touchdown run and 18-yard scoring pass to Carlos Carson gave the Chiefs a 42–31 lead with 11:04 left in the fourth quarter. The Seahawks made it 42–38 on Warner's third touchdown run and

SEAHAWKS CAREER RUSHING LEADERS

Yards	Player
8,713	Shaun Alexander (2000–present)
6,706	Chris Warren (1990–97)
6,705	Curt Warner (1983–89)

NFL CAREER RUSHING TOUCHDOWN LEADERS

	Player	TDs	Seasons
1.	Emmitt Smith	164	15
2.	Marcus Allen	123	16
3.	Walter Payton	110	13
4.	Jim Brown	106	9
5.	John Riggins	104	14
6.	Marshall Faulk	100	13
6.	LaDainian Tomlinson	100	6
8.	Barry Sanders	99	10
9.	Shaun Alexander	96	7
10.	Franco Harris	91	13
10.	Jerome Bettis	91	12

took a 45–42 lead on Krieg's 14-yard pass to Paul Johns on fourth-and-6 with 2:21 remaining.

Kenney responded by directing the Chiefs 80 yards on six plays and hitting former Seahawk Theotis Brown with a 21-yard touchdown throw with 90 seconds left. But instead of a four-point lead, the Chiefs had to settle for a 48–45 margin when Nick Lowery's extra-point attempt went wide left.

The Seahawks moved the ball into Johnson's range, and the kicker sent the game into overtime. Johnson quickly got another shot as Dixon took the overtime kickoff back 47 yards to the Kansas City 48-yard line, and Warner gained 24 yards on three carries to set Johnson up for the game-winning and record-setting points.

Including the shootout at the Dome, the Seahawks won three of their final four games on the way to the first playoff berth in team history and a postseason run that would not end until they lost to the division-rival Raiders in the AFC title game.

"WE WANT THE BALL, AND WE'RE GONNA SCORE!"

Matt Hasselbeck's bravado seemed well-founded just before the Seahawks took the ball in overtime at Lambeau Field on January 4, 2004. After all, the Seahawks had just driven down the field to tie the score and send the NFC wild-card playoff game into overtime. But Al Harris made Hasselbeck eat his words when he returned one of the quarterback's passes for a touchdown on Seattle's second drive of the extra period, sending the Seahawks packing with a 33–27 loss.

But not lost in the defeat was the emergence of Hasselbeck as the Seahawks' franchise quarterback. On a day the opposing defense focused on shutting down Shaun Alexander, Hasselbeck dueled Brett Favre, his former mentor and a three-time league MVP, to a virtual draw. Each threw for over 300 yards, moving their teams up and down the field in a back-and-forth battle.

Hasselbeck engineered a 63-yard drive to tie the score with 51 seconds left. Shaun Alexander did the honors, setting a team playoff record with his third rushing touchdown. Favre nearly trumped Hasselbeck by driving the Packers to the Seattle 29-yard line with five seconds left, but Ryan Longwell's 47-yard field goal came up short in the 20-degree cold of Lambeau.

When the captains came out for the overtime coin toss, the Seahawks won, and Hasselbeck uttered his infamous—and, as it turned out, erroneous—guarantee. Not knowing the official's microphone was on and his words were about to be heard by a national television audience, the confident quarterback told the official and his former Packers teammates, "We want the ball, and we're gonna score!"

The teams each went three-and-out on their first overtime series, and on the fifth play of Seattle's second possession, Hasselbeck's pass to the left was intercepted by Harris and

Green Bay Packers cornerback Al Harris heads to the end zone in front of Seahawks receiver Alex Bannister in overtime of their NFC wild-card playoff game on January 4, 2004, in Green Bay. Harris returned an interception for the game-winning touchdown in the Packers 33–27 win.

returned 52 yards. It came on a play in which Hasselbeck called an audible, and the quarterback said later that he should have thrown the ball away.

The teams exchanged field goals for most of the first half, with Josh Brown hitting from 30 and 35 yards and Longwell knocking them in from 31 and 27 yards. The Packers led 13–6 at halftime on the strength of Favre's 23-yard touchdown pass to tight end Bubba Franks.

The second half turned into a shootout, with Favre and Hasselbeck gunning their teams down the field and Alexander and Ahman Green finishing things off with a total of five one-yard touchdown runs. Alexander's first touchdown tied the score at 13 on the first drive of the third quarter, and then Hasselbeck picked apart the Packers' secondary to set up another one-yard plunge by Alexander. The Packers responded with a pair of scores by Green, the latter giving Green Bay a 27–20 lead with 2:44 remaining in the fourth quarter. Then Hasselbeck took the Seahawks 63 yards in seven plays, ending in Alexander's third score.

It was the Seahawks' second loss at Lambeau Field that season, and Coach Holmgren—who had led the Packers to two Super Bowls and one title in the 1990s—took it hard.

"To be honest with you, I'm dying inside—it hurts bad to lose this game today," he told reporters. "The locker room is in bad shape right now."

A COMEBACK FUMBLED

In December 1999 the Seahawks were in a free fall. An 8–2 start had disintegrated into an 8–5 record, and their playoff prospects were rapidly evaporating with every loss.

It was against that backdrop that the Seahawks proceeded to play one of the wildest games they had ever been involved in against the Denver Broncos, a Rocky Mountain roller-coaster ride that alternately looked to be a sure loss and then a seeming miracle comeback before ending in a bizarre, demoralizing defeat.

The Broncos seemed to have it all in hand after Olandis Gary had run for 183 yards against the Seahawks and Jon Kitna had fumbled twice to set up Denver scores. Gary's 71-yard run had set up Brian Griese's nine-yard touchdown pass to tight end Dwayne Carswell with 1:47 left, and the Broncos' 30–20 lead looked good enough for many of the fans, who began to stream out of frigid Mile High Stadium.

But the Seahawks were not finished. Kitna proceeded to march the offense down the field, throwing a 36-yard touchdown pass to Derrick Mayes with 54 seconds left. Todd Peterson then popped a perfect onside kick, which Kerry Joseph caught to set up a chance to tie the score. Kitna hit Sean Dawkins for 26 yards, and Peterson nailed a 45-yard field goal with nine seconds to go, setting Seattle up for one of the biggest comebacks in franchise history.

When Denver failed to get a first down after winning the overtime coin toss, the Seahawks had gained all of the momentum, and many thought the miracle victory was all but assured. Kitna began to drive the offense down the field, hitting Dawkins for 17 yards on third down. But, a play after Kitna overthrew a wide-open Joey Galloway for what would have been the winning score, the game was ended by the Broncos.

On third down, with five receivers in the pattern, the Seahawks were unable to stop blitzing cornerback Ray Crockett from sacking Kitna and causing a fumble, which Denver's Glenn Cadrez returned 37 yards for a 36–30 victory—just the second time in NFL history an overtime game had been decided by a fumble return for a touchdown.

Just like that, Seattle's miracle comeback had ended in a fourth straight loss that was by far the most demoralizing of the streak.

Denver Broncos cornerback Ray Crockett hits John Kitna to knock the ball loose and allow Broncos linebacker Glenn Cadrez to recover the fumble and score a game-winning touchdown in the Broncos' 36–30 overtime victory on December 19, 1999.

"They have all been difficult, but this was a very emotional ending," Coach Holmgren told reporters. "There were quite a lot of mood swings, so in the locker room it's a tough thing. You think you have a chance to win the game, and then in a blink it's over. That's tough."

The loss dropped the Seahawks a game behind the Kansas City Chiefs in the AFC West, setting up essentially a one-game playoff for the division title when the teams played the following week.

"Our playoffs have started," Kitna told reporters. "We've been asking for a playoff game around here for 10 years…. It's do or die."

The Seahawks ended up beating Kansas City 23–14 and backing into the division title the next week when both teams lost.

KICKED WHILE THEY WERE DOWN

When Robbie Gould's 49-yard field goal sailed straight through the uprights to give Chicago a 27–24 overtime win in a divisional playoff game at Soldier Field, it was in some ways a merciful end to a very painful 2006 season for the Seahawks.

The Seahawks—decimated by injuries throughout the season—had been lucky just to get to the divisional playoffs. It surprised many national observers that they were even able to take the NFC's best team to overtime. But when they did, they fell prey to the weaknesses that had stalked them all season—an inability to convert short-yardage situations and a failure to stop big pass plays. And with that, they fell two wins short of a follow-up appearance in the Super Bowl.

Matt Hasselbeck, who had missed four games with a sprained knee and played the rest of the way with broken fingers on his left (non-throwing) hand, summed up the season simply to reporters after the game: "This was not our year."

Even with that, Seattle had a chance to make its second straight NFC Championship Game. Shaun Alexander ran for 108 yards and two touchdowns, giving Seattle a 24–21 lead with a 13-yard scoring run up the middle in the third quarter. And even

RUNNING HISTORY

The Seahawks were there for Walter Payton's final home game in 1987 (Seattle beat Chicago 34–21). Payton's death on November 1, 1999, overshadowed a Monday night game in which Mike Holmgren went back to Green Bay in his first season as coach of the Seahawks. Holmgren's Seahawks also were on the field when Emmitt Smith surpassed Payton as the NFL's career rushing leader on October 27, 2002, in Dallas. That was the day Matt Hasselbeck replaced an injured Trent Dilfer as Seattle's starting quarterback for good. Although Smith got the record, the Seahawks beat the Cowboys 17–14.

after Gould had tied it at 24 early in the fourth quarter, the Seahawks had several more opportunities.

But the Seattle offense failed to convert key downs late in the game and in overtime. Part of it can be attributed to yet another injury: Pro Bowl fullback Mack Strong, who was the only offensive player along with left tackle Walter Jones to play in every game, left this game with pinched nerves that had made his right arm useless. That hindered the short-yardage effort behind a line that featured two first-year starters—rookie left guard Rob Sims and second-year center Chris Spencer.

With two minutes left in regulation, Alexander was stopped on third-and-one at the Chicago 44-yard line. Seattle went for it, but Hasselbeck bobbled the snap and Alexander was stuffed for a two-yard loss by Lance Briggs. The Seahawks got the ball back again with 1:38 to go, and Alexander gained 27 of Seattle's 35 yards as the Seahawks drove to Chicago's 45-yard line with 30 seconds left. The Seahawks needed only five yards to get in field-goal position for Josh Brown, who had hit four game-winning kicks that season and whose career long was 58 yards. But rather than run the red-hot Alexander to try to get those five yards, the Seahawks threw the ball.

Hasselbeck spiked the ball on first down to stop the clock. On second down Hasselbeck threw an incompletion down the right sideline to Deion Branch. Then Hasselbeck dropped back to pass again and—unable to find a receiver for nearly five seconds—allowed himself to be sacked for a nine-yard loss. A fourth-down pass fell incomplete, and the game went into overtime.

Receiving the ball first, the Seahawks moved it to their 48-yard line before having to punt, and rookie Ryan Plackemeier was pressured into pooching an 18-yarder that was the shortest punt in overtime of an NFL playoff game. On third-and-10, Chicago quarterback Rex Grossman found an unchecked Rashied Davis for a 30-yard pass against a Seattle secondary playing without three of its top four cornerbacks. Four plays later Gould split the uprights with the second-longest kick in NFL postseason history.

Alexander acknowledged that the Seahawks had their chances and did not take advantage, telling reporters, "You could second-guess everything, but the truth is that we gave it everything we had and we fell short."

Holmgren was optimistic his team would recover, telling reporters, "It's a tough one, but we have a good core of players. The organization is healthy. And I hope down the road we get a few more cracks at this thing."

THE ARBITERS HAVE IT

THE BOGUS CALL THAT CHANGED IT ALL

It was not only one of the worst calls in NFL history, it was a play that changed the way the NFL officiated its games and a moment that arguably altered the Seahawks franchise forever.

On December 6, 1998, Vinny Testaverde was awarded a touchdown on a fourth-down run on which he was tackled almost a full yard short of the end zone, and the New York Jets squashed the Seahawks' playoff hopes with an ill-gotten 32–31 victory at the Meadowlands.

With the Jets facing a fourth down from the Seahawks' 5-yard line with 27 seconds left, Testaverde ran for the end zone and was tackled almost a yard short by Jay Bellamy and Cortez Kennedy. But head linesman Earnie Frantz signaled touchdown, and referee Phil Luckett let the call stand without consulting with his other officials even though it was obvious that the only thing that had crossed the goal line was Testaverde's helmet; the ball was down around his midsection, nearly a full yard away from the end zone.

"Because he had signaled a touchdown, so far as we're concerned, it's over," a mistaken Luckett told a reporter afterward.

The Seahawks were incensed. Cornerback Shawn Springs threw his helmet in disgust, garnering a penalty for unsportsmanlike conduct.

"Most definitely, he wasn't in," Bellamy told reporters. "Let the players who are playing decide the game. That was our season."

New York Jets tackle Jason Fabini signals a touchdown after quarterback Vinny Testaverde crossed the goal line—with his helmet, but not the ball— to score on a five-yard run late in the fourth quarter against the Seahawks on December 6, 1998, in East Rutherford, New Jersey.

Indeed it was. The Seahawks missed the postseason by one win in 1998, a finish that spelled the end for coach Dennis Erickson, who was fired after compiling a 31–33 record in four years and failing to get Seattle into the playoffs.

The foul-up by Luckett's crew was the most grievous error in a 1998 season that had been chock full of officiating problems. Luckett himself had been at the center of controversy on Thanksgiving when he misheard Jerome Bettis's call during an overtime coin toss and wrongly awarded the ball to Detroit, which immediately drove for the winning field goal.

Luckett's incompetence was a driving force for the return of instant replay the next season. The review system, which had been used from 1986 to 1991, had been denied by two votes before the 1998 season. But it was reinstated for the 1999 season with a coaches' challenge system that is still used today.

Mike Holmgren, who replaced Erickson in Seattle in 1999, was a key figure in promoting instant replay through the NFL's competition committee, and he told reporters that the Testaverde touchdown was one of the plays that made some owners change their minds about the use of instant replay.

Meanwhile, three weeks after the Jets game, and after the Seahawks had finished 8–8 for the third time in Erickson's four seasons, the team relieved the coach. Holmgren was hired less than two weeks later, and he used the remnants of Erickson's club to make the playoffs in 1999 before rebuilding the team to his standards and turning it into a perennial playoff participant beginning in 2003. (Coincidentally, the Seahawks backed into the playoffs in 1999 despite a loss in the season finale at the hands of—who else?—the Jets.)

Thus from one of the worst calls in NFL history came one of the best things to happen to both the NFL and the Seahawks—the return of instant replay and the hiring of the coach who eventually would take the Seahawks to their first Super Bowl.

As Paul Moyer, a longtime Seahawks safety/coach/broadcaster, said, "It hurt the team short term, but it was the greatest thing long term that ever happened to the franchise because we get Holmgren and a pretty good group of people running the franchise."

SCORE ONE FOR THE REFS

An 0–3 start in 1990 pretty much doomed the Seahawks to missing the playoffs for the second straight year. But if they could have gotten one more win, they would have been in. And that's where the refs got in the way.

After being shut out in the first game of the season in Chicago, the Seahawks came back to the Kingdome for their first meeting that season with the Los Angeles Raiders, and instead of walking away with a 17–10 victory, they ended up losing 17–13 thanks to two bad calls by the referees.

The first gaffe came with Seattle leading 10–3 in the third quarter. On a third-down play, the Raiders' Jay Schroeder completed a 45-yard pass to Mervyn Fernandez down to the Seattle 32-yard line. The receiver did not get both feet in bounds, but the officials did not pause to review the obviously close play.

Replay official Bob Beeks thought the field referee, Jerry Markbreit, had stopped play so he could examine the tape. So he didn't call down to tell him they were reviewing it. But the play had been called a completion, and Markbreit did not know Beeks was reviewing it so he let the Raiders run the next play, which by rule meant the previous play could not be overturned. The Raiders went on to tie the score five plays later.

Markbreit explained to a reporter: "The play was ruled complete from the field. We got nothing from replay. We naturally assumed the play is OK.... [The Raiders] snapped the ball, and that was it."

Seahawks coach Chuck Knox could not believe the officials had missed such an obvious incompletion—twice.

"Fernandez did not come down with both feet in bounds," Knox told reporters. "There wasn't any question about it. You'd have liked to have thought that the referee could say, 'Hey, there's something wrong and make sure we get this right. This is too critical.'"

Fernandez even admitted after the game that he had one foot out of bounds.

In the fourth quarter, with the game still tied 10–10, John L. Williams was denied a touchdown by the officials even though he had extended the ball over the plane of the goal line. The Seahawks ended up kicking a field goal to take a 13–10 lead with 6:07 remaining.

The two missed calls allowed the Raiders to win the game with their last-minute, 65-yard touchdown drive; Greg Bell ran it in from the 1-yard line with 1:26 left.

"That was a tough one to take," Knox told reporters. "It's one thing to get beat but…"

It's another to have that loss cost you a playoff spot. Because of the referees' errors in the second week of the season, the Seahawks finished 9–7 rather than 10–6 in a season in which 10 wins would have put them in the AFC playoffs, ahead of the Houston Oilers (9–7).

THE SUPER BOWL—XL CONTROVERSY

One lampoon cartoon of Super Bowl XL depicted referees wearing the black and gold colors of the Pittsburgh Steelers and throwing the Steelers' famed Terrible Towels instead of the usual yellow flags used for penalties. It was an apropos commentary on perhaps the most controversial Super Bowl in the 40 games that had been played under that title.

It was fitting that the Seahawks' first NFL title game was called Super Bowl XL, because it turned into an extra-large controversy. The Seahawks, their fans, and almost everyone outside of Pittsburgh believed the Seahawks didn't get a fair deal on February

IF ONLY...

The Seahawks played a key role in the 1999 return of instant replay. In a December 1998 game against the Jets, New York quarterback Vinny Testaverde was awarded a late touchdown on a scramble into the end zone, giving the Jets a 32–31 win. Replays showed that Testaverde was tackled well short of the end zone, however. The loss cost the Seahawks a spot in the playoffs.

5, 2006. Five huge plays went against the Seahawks, who couldn't overcome the questionable calls in a 21–10 loss to the Steelers.

It started early. In the first quarter, Darrell Jackson was called for pass interference against Pittsburgh safety Chris Hope even though both players were engaged in hand fighting. The call came in the end zone after Jackson had caught a pass that would have been the first touchdown of the game. Hope complained, and the official threw the flag late.

On the first play of the second quarter, a 34-yard punt return by Peter Warrick was called back when Etric Pruitt was called for holding. The penalty left the Seahawks at their 25-yard line instead of at the Steelers' 46. The holding was not evident on any review, and Coach Holmgren later told *Sports Illustrated*, "That's the call that really still bugs me. We're up 3–0 and could have had a very short field to try to go up 10–0, and we get a really, really, really, really tick-tack call like that. That's a killer."

Matt Hasselbeck puts up his hands in surrender after several big calls go against the Seahawks in Super Bowl XL against the Pittsburgh Steelers on February 5, 2006.

Holmgren was even more incensed about Pittsburgh's touchdown with two minutes left in the half. Quarterback Ben Roethlisberger appeared to come up short of the end zone on a third-down dive, and head linesman Mark Hittner seemed to signal fourth down by raising his right arm. But, after Roethlisberger stretched the ball forward, Hittner raised his other arm to signal touchdown. Referee Bill Leavy upheld the call on a replay review because the video did not conclusively show where the football was when Roethlisberger went down. Holmgren argued this play vehemently with Leavy as he went to the locker room for halftime with his team trailing 7–3.

With about 12 minutes left and Seattle trailing 14–10, the Seahawks were on the wrong end of another crucial judgment call when right tackle Sean Locklear was called for holding on a play in which Matt Hasselbeck hit Jerramy Stevens for an 18-yard gain to the Pittsburgh 1-yard line. Locklear had let Clark Haggans come upfield in a move used by every tackle in the league, and the referee thought Locklear had hooked Haggans. The play wiped out Seattle's best chance to take the lead and was the straw that broke the camel's back for Hasselbeck.

Three plays later, the admittedly disturbed quarterback threw an interception. And the referees piled on with the most glaringly inaccurate call of the day by calling the quarterback for an illegal block while he was tackling Ike Taylor. It was a ridiculous call, considering Hasselbeck wasn't blocking anyone and was in fact a defender making a tackle. The call gave the Steelers an extra 15 yards, which helped as they quickly capitalized with a touchdown pass from Antwaan Randle El to Hines Ward.

The Seahawks had two more opportunities to try to overcome the 21–10 deficit, but they couldn't do it. And the referees made yet another bad call when they ruled Hasselbeck had lost the ball on a fumble at his 16-yard line with less than nine minutes left. The Seahawks had to challenge via instant replay to retain possession.

The Seahawks, for the most part, refused to blame the referees for the team's loss in its first Super Bowl. But Jackson and Holmgren made it clear the Seahawks did not agree with everything the officials did.

"We made our plays," Jackson told reporters. "But somehow, some way, we had them called back."

A day after the game, in a rally at Qwest Field, Holmgren shared the fans' frustration when he told the crowd, "I knew it would be tough going against the Pittsburgh Steelers, but I didn't know we were going to have to play the guys in the striped shirts as well."

The NFL defended its officials in the immediate aftermath of the game, saying the Super Bowl had been officiated properly. Everyone figured Holmgren would be handed a large fine for his critical comments regarding the officials, so it was very telling when commissioner Paul Tagliabue tore up the disciplinary letter that sat on his desk several months later. His actions spoke volumes about what the league really thought about the officiating.

> **DID YOU KNOW...**
>
> The Seahawks only had seven penalties in Super Bowl XL, but it seemed as though every one occurred at a pivotal point in the game.

All but Roethlisberger's touchdown were judgment calls, but they were judgments that often are not made and that were very one-sided. Holmgren's Seahawks had always been one of the least-penalized teams in the NFL—that season they had just 94 penalties, tied for second fewest in the league. But in the Super Bowl, they were called for seven fouls that cost them 70 yards and two touchdowns, while the Steelers were penalized just three times for 20 yards.

In May 2006 the Seahawks finally had a chance to air their gripes against the league for the way they were treated in the Super Bowl. Mike Peireira, the NFL's chief of officials, visited Seahawks headquarters in his annual meeting with teams to discuss rules changes for the upcoming season.

"Mike was fair, he was good, and we agreed to disagree on a few things," Holmgren told *Sports Illustrated*. "It went fine. But there are a few things that happened in that game that we wouldn't agree on if we both lived to be 100."

THE 12ᵀᴴ MAN

Just before the final game of a 1984 season that would end with a franchise-record 12 wins and a second consecutive playoff berth, the Seahawks made an unprecedented move: they became the first professional sports franchise to retire a jersey number in honor of their fans.

The retirement of No. 12—in honor of the 12th Man—was a well-earned tribute to the deafening denizens of the Kingdome, who had loudly cheered their team since its inception in 1976. In fact, it was one of those raucous fans, Randy Ford, who had proposed the idea to the Seahawks.

"It was a worthy tribute to fans of the Seahawks," said Hall of Fame receiver Steve Largent. "There's very few teams that have the kind of support that we have had over the years."

The power of the 12th Man was on display throughout the 1980s, when the Kingdome shook with the shouts of more than 60,000 fans every game. There is no better example of the fans' influence than in Seattle's 35–27 win over the Los Angeles Raiders on *Monday Night Football* in 1988. At one point in that game, the Raiders were called for illegal procedure five times in a row because the crowd was so loud that the L.A. players couldn't hear the quarterback.

"It was such a great benefit," former quarterback Dave Krieg said. "You'd be on the sideline, and the place would be deafening. It would send chills down your spine. On the flip side, they would boo very loud when something went wrong, and that would send chills down your spine the other way."

The defensive guys loved it, too, even if it made it harder for them to communicate.

"It made it really difficult for me because I was calling the huddle and making adjustments," middle linebacker Dave Wyman said. "We had to use hand signals, run up and tap people on the butt. There were a lot of things we couldn't do. It did hamper us a little bit. But what more than made up for it was the adrenaline rush.... You could practically float off the field, it was so inspiring."

The players laughed at the lengths to which teams would go to prepare to play in the cacophonous Kingdome. Using stereo

The Seahawks have built up a rabid fan base over the years that has become a distinct advantage over visiting teams.

systems turned up to full volume during practice, having linemen hold hands to avoid false starts, quarterbacks using the silent count and lifting a leg when they wanted the center to snap the ball.

"We'd be reading about what they were going to do. It was always something new," safety Paul Moyer said. "Everybody complained, the Raiders the most, it seemed."

"And then they would get there, and it would be a lot worse than what they had practiced for," nose tackle Joe Nash chuckled. "It helped us in a lot of situations."

Apparently NFL owners thought fans at the Kingdome and elsewhere were helping too much, because in March 1989 the owners passed a rule that would penalize excessively loud crowds that disrupted the ability of visiting offenses to call their plays. The owners had been considering the noise rule since 1983, which not so coincidentally is the year the Seahawks started really giving their fans something to cheer about. But it did not pass until the Minnesota Vikings, of all teams, changed their vote to *yes*, giving the necessary 21–7 edge needed to pass any measure. In fact, the Vikings were among three of the league's six dome teams who voted in favor of the rule, which enabled referees to dock timeouts and then assess five-yard penalties against home teams whose fans were so loud that the opposing quarterback could not call the play.

Needless to say, Seahawks coach Chuck Knox was not pleased by the vote, telling *USA Today*, "I just don't want to take away our fans' right to participate in the game."

The first instance of the rule being enforced came, of course, at the Kingdome. In a preseason game on September 1, 1989, San Francisco quarterback Steve Young's pleas to referee Red Cashion resulted in the Seahawks losing three timeouts. The 49ers were poised at the Seahawks' 2-yard line, and the Kingdome crowd was in its usual frenzy in an attempt to help its defense. Young stepped away from center three times, and Cashion threw the flag every time because the crowd just got more fired up at the insult of being penalized for supporting its defense.

"We're trying to get them to tone it down, and they are getting louder," Moyer said. "How can you penalize 67,000 people?"

As the Seahawks were preparing for the 1989 season opener in Philadelphia, Knox once again voiced his disdain for the noise rule.

"You know," Knox told reporters, "Paul Brown [owner of the Cincinnati Bengals] voted for the rule because the Bengals got to go to Cleveland once a year and they've got those dawgs in the end zones that bark and howl and throw bones out on the field. Maybe they ought to have a rule for throwing dog bones. And what about in Denver, where they pelt you with snowballs. How about a snowball rule?"

(It was incredibly ironic that three months later snowballs would be a problem for the Seahawks not in Denver but in Brown's own stadium in Cincinnati. And that Sam Wyche would chastise his home crowd with the ultimate insult of comparing them to Cleveland's Dawg Pound.)

Knox said the owners probably didn't know what kind of mess they were creating when they voted for the noise rule.

"I think there was some confusion at that meeting," he said. "That might be an understatement. There probably was a lot of confusion. But nothing like the confusion that's going to follow that thing around."

Knox's criticism might have found an ear in the league office because, two days later, commissioner Pete Rozelle created his own amendment to the rule, telling his referees they could penalize the offense if the quarterback refused to run a play when the referee thought it was quiet enough to do so. Rozelle told his officials to use discretion when judging crowd noise and deciding whether to penalize the home team.

As a result, in the first week of the season, the only noise-related penalty called was a delay of game against Kansas City quarterback Steve DeBerg, who ran out of time because Cashion refused to throw a flag for a noise violation in Denver.

Quarterbacks all over the league tried to take advantage of the noise rule that season, but, as Knox pointed out, Rozelle had effectively vetoed the new rule.

During Seattle's 24–21 overtime loss to Denver at the Kingdome in October 1989, John Elway stepped away from center three times, and referee Johnny Grier warned the Kingdome crowd each time but did not penalize the Seahawks. On one play after Grier told Elway to continue play, Elway was sacked by Seattle's speedy pass rusher, Rufus Porter.

The boisterous Kingdome crowd had always helped Seattle's speed rushers. Jacob Green once said the home fans were responsible for as many as 50 of his 116 career sacks. Porter, who played with Green for four years, also credited the home fans for many of his 41 sacks—35 of which came from 1989 to 1992.

"The Kingdome was such a huge advantage because it made average people great," Moyer said. "It made Rufus Porter a great pass rusher. It made Jacob Green better than he was. It gave an advantage to undersized guys with quickness."

After Porter ravaged the Cincinnati Bengals in a Monday night game in 1990, Wyche credited the Kingdome fans, telling reporters, "The fans were great to Seattle and not abusive to us, but obviously there is no crowd noise rule anymore." Although it

DIE HARDS

For nine seasons, the Seahawks' defensive line consisted of Jacob Green, Joe Nash, and Jeff Bryant. From 1983 to 1989, they were the front men for Seattle's 3-4 defense. And in 1990 and 1991, they were joined by Cortez Kennedy. The three J's played together so long that they began to call themselves the Die Hards, after the battery of the same name. The name came about after one practice during training camp in which injuries forced the three starters to work for all but one snap the entire session. "You'd have to drag us off the field to get us out," Nash said. "We were playing 75 plays a game. We just didn't want to come out."

was rarely applied after 1989, the noise rule remained on the books until it quietly was killed by NFL owners in March 2007.

Kingdome attendance waned in the 1990s as the Seahawks failed to record a winning season for eight straight years. And Husky Stadium, where the Seahawks played in 2000 and 2001, was no advantage whatsoever. Neither was Qwest Field in its early days. When the facility opened under the moniker Seahawks Stadium in 2002, it drew big crowds to every game. Unfortunately, many of the fans wore the opposing team's color.

In June 2003 Seahawks owner Paul Allen hired Tod Leiweke as CEO, charging the longtime sports executive with rebuilding the Seahawks' image and bringing back the fans. One of the first things Leiweke did was introduce the 12th Man flag, a large pennant bearing the No. 12 in honor of the fans. Leiweke began to bring back former Seahawks to raise the standard in the south end zone before each game.

Over the next two seasons, the fans began to return, and by the time Mike Holmgren's Seahawks had ascended to Super Bowl contenders in 2005, Qwest Field was rocking as loudly as the Kingdome ever had. It was so loud in one game in 2005 that the New York Giants were called for 11 false starts.

And just before the Giants returned in September 2006, the league dispatched someone to monitor the noise at Qwest Field amid concerns that the Seahawks were piping in artificial sound. Teams such as the Vikings had used the tactic before.

Holmgren said unequivocally that the Seahawks do not enhance the noise level, and he said he hoped the fans would take the implication as an insult and show the Giants and the NFL what loud really was. "If I'm a fan," he said, "I take that personally, like, 'If you think last game was loud, or you think the NFC Championship Game was loud, wait until Sunday.'"

Quarterback Matt Hasselbeck said fans should consider it a compliment that some thought it was impossible for them to be so loud, and he encouraged them to be even louder.

In 2005 and 2006, the Seahawks produced more false-start penalties from opponents at Qwest Field than any other team did on its home field. Seattle led the league in both years with a combined 50 such penalties—an average of more than three per game and 12 more than the next-highest team, the Vikings, who played in the Metrodome.

Giants defensive end Michael Strahan played in the Kingdome in 1995, when the Seahawks were coming off three horrendous years under Tom Flores and the fan base had shrunk as a result. It was not the Kingdome of the 1980s and early 1990s, so Strahan had no experience with the noise at the Seahawks' old facility. But he could well judge Qwest Field against fields around the league, and he was impressed.

"Loudest stadium I've ever been to, without a doubt," Strahan told reporters in 2006. "The amazing thing is it's an outdoor stadium. I don't know if it's the way that they designed it or whatever. It is the loudest place. You can barely hear yourself talk. You can barely hear yourself think, actually. That's one of the other challenges. It's not just you against the Seahawks. This truly is a 12th man–type situation where you're playing against the fans, too."

RIVALRIES

BEST OF THE AFC WEST

When the Seahawks joined the AFC West in 1977—after spending their first season in the NFC West—they immediately became the ugly stepchild. They were the unwanted baby in a family that had been together since 1963, and that's how they often were treated on the field for the next 25 years.

The NFL didn't even consider them a true member of the division, because the league yanked them out of the AFC West in 2002 and put them in the new NFC West.

The Seahawks had plenty of trouble in their old division, amassing a dismal 80–110 record against the Denver Broncos, Kansas City Chiefs, Oakland/L.A. Raiders, and San Diego Chargers. The Hawks won barely a third of their games against the Broncos (17–32) and Chiefs (17–30) and also had a losing record against the Raiders (22–26). The Chargers were the only team they could beat more than half the time (24–22), and they could thank the Chargers' terrible defense in the 1980s and Rian Lindell in the 2000s for that.

There were times when the Seahawks could hardly be called *rivals* of their AFC West foes—like when the Seahawks started 0–8 against the Chargers. Or when they lost eight straight in Kansas City in the 1980s and then went 1–14 against the Chiefs during the 1990s. Or when they went 6–18 against the Broncos from 1989 to 2000. Or when they lost eight straight to the Raiders in the early 1990s.

Of course, all of those losses made the wins so much more meaningful. Like the first one against the Chargers, which opened the floodgates for 12 wins in the next 14 games against San Diego. Like sweeping the Raiders and Broncos in 1983 and 1988 and beating both in the playoffs. And like ending that 10-year losing streak in Kansas City on Dave Krieg's final-play touchdown pass to Paul Skansi.

"It was a great division to play in. We saw the rise and fall of many teams," said Hall of Fame receiver Steve Largent, who had great battles against the Raiders' Lester Hayes and Mike Haynes and two very memorable games against the Broncos in 1988. "It was a special time to play because the AFC had great teams."

Bronco Busters

When the Seahawks made their surprise run to the AFC title game in 1983, their first playoff opponent was the Denver Broncos. Krieg threw three touchdown passes in Seattle's easy 31–7 win, but he remembers the game for another reason.

The Broncos benched starting quarterback Steve DeBerg in the fourth quarter, and Krieg watched "some young kid come in and start zipping the ball around. And I'm thinking, 'They should have started that guy.' That was my first look at John Elway."

Elway, the number one pick in the draft that year, had not played against the Seahawks in the two regular-season meetings. But he completed 10 of 15 passes for 123 yards in half a quarter of the playoff game.

"He was like Dave Krieg in a Maserati," said linebacker Dave Wyman, who had played with Elway at Stanford and respected Krieg's leadership and competitiveness enough to make that statement a compliment. "[Elway had] the same competitive attitude, always so driven, but his physical attributes were outstanding."

"We used to call him the freak," nose tackle Joe Nash said. "The things that he did were freakish. We were in awe of some of the things he would do. He was a lot faster than [his 40-yard time] when he ran.

The Seahawks' Chris Canty takes down Denver Broncos returner Chris Watson in a typically hard-hitting game between the two Western Division rivals.

"Throwing the ball from one side of the field to the other when we thought we had him cornered, he was like Harry Houdini sometimes."

Wyman recalled his first game as a rookie in 1987, having to go in for an injured Fredd Young. "I looked like Don Knotts with knees knocking, and Elway looks at me and winks at me. He had such confidence, a swagger, knowing he was going to win."

Elway won that game, throwing for 321 yards and getting the best of Seattle's notorious rookie linebacker, Brian Bosworth, in a 40–17 blowout. That was Denver's fifth win in six meetings.

PARCELLS IN PASSING

The Seahawks faced Bill Parcells in his first and last games as coach of the New York Jets (in 1997 and 1999, Seattle lost both) and in his last game with the Dallas Cowboys (Seattle won in the 2006 playoffs). They also faced the coach in his first season with the New York Giants (1983, Seattle won) and twice in his first year with the New England Patriots (1993, Seattle won both).

The Seahawks made up for that loss by beating the Broncos 28–21 at home toward the end of the season. The win was key in getting the Seahawks into the playoffs in the strike-marred year.

The 1988 season opener in Denver was one of the most eventful games in the series—a contest Seattle won 21–14.

Wyman, making his first start, had a huge collision with tight end Clarence Kay on a running play. Kay's helmet smashed Wyman in the chin, and the linebacker fell to the ground just in time to recover a fumble by Tony Dorsett. While getting his chin stapled shut on the sideline, Wyman figured he had taken the worst of the crash until he looked back onto the field and saw Kay being hauled off on a stretcher. Wyman had been so woozy from the hit that he didn't know Kay had been out on his feet.

"It was a hard-hitting game," Wyman said in simple understatement.

The hardest hit came from a Denver safety whose name, appropriately, was Mike Harden. His helmet-breaking, teeth-loosening, fine-inducing hit knocked Largent out before he found the grass and set up one of the greatest payback moments in sports history three months later (recounted in chapter 1).

"It was a nasty hit," Wyman said, adding that it looked like Harden was trying to make up for "the frustration of every defensive back that was 10 times faster than Steve and a better athlete than Steve but had gotten burned by him a million times."

After they swept the Broncos in 1988, the Seahawks had a tough time beating Elway's team, going 7–19 through their final season in the AFC West (2001). The two best victories were the overtime win in 1992, when the Seahawks inducted Pete Gross into the Ring of Honor and then got just their second win of a 2–14 season, and in 1995, when the Hawks rallied from a 20–0 deficit to win 31–27.

One of the Seahawks' most bizarre losses during that stretch came in October 1989, when Denver won 24–21 in overtime on a terrible day for kicking teams. David Treadwell and Norm Johnson took turns trying to be the goat. The Denver kicker missed three field goals, including a 27-yard attempt with nine seconds left in regulation. And then Johnson missed a 40-yarder in overtime—on second down—to set up Treadwell's winning 27-yard field goal. The Seahawks also botched a 36-yard field-goal try when center Grant Feasel snapped the ball while holder Jeff Kemp wasn't looking, hitting the quarterback in the helmet. The punch line to this joke of a game was Seattle punter Ruben Rodriguez, who boomed a punt minus-two yards. He had a tough time explaining how a punt could travel backwards *inside the Kingdome.*

Raider Haters

Some of the Seahawks' best wins came against the ever-hated Raiders, who disliked the upstart Seahawks just as much.

It started early. In November 1978 Efren Herrera nailed a 46-yard field goal with three seconds left to give Seattle a 17–16 win and the first season sweep of the Raiders by any team since 1965. The Seahawks then swept them again in 1979.

After losing five straight, the Seahawks swept the Raiders again in 1983, including a 38–36 win at the Kingdome in which Seattle created eight turnovers and had eight sacks. The Raiders got even in the AFC Championship Game, punishing the upstart Seahawks 30–14 behind 154 rushing yards by Marcus Allen.

"They kind of intimidated us," Krieg said. "They drank more than just coffee to get ready for that game."

Krieg said it took a few games to get over the Raiders mystique. "They were always tough guys and bullies, and they had that intimidating factor."

Seahawks players learned early on that the Raiders' aura of intimidation worked more in the stands than on the football field.

In one of the 1984 games, Krieg remembers "a big white jersey coming at me. I'm going to get hit, and it's going to hurt. The hit drove my shoulder in the ground. But I got up and went back to the huddle. I had kind of faced the [Raiders] demons. You had to meet the bully."

The Seahawks turned bully on the Raiders in a wild-card playoff game that season. The Seahawks, who had played most of the year without running back Curt Warner, were missing starting left tackle Ron Essink and threw just 10 passes as Dan Doornink ran for 123 yards and the defense recorded six sacks and three turnovers in a 13–7 win.

"It was another one of those Ground Chuck–type games where we ran it more than we threw it," Largent said.

By the mid-1980s, the Raiders mystique had begun to fade a bit.

"The Raiders were always very funny because they were so about intimidation; they were bad asses," Wyman said. "That worked with fans, but to other players it's funny: 'We're supposed to be afraid of you?'"

The Seahawks certainly weren't scared in December 1986, when they recorded a team-record 11 sacks in a 37–0 victory on *Monday Night Football*. It was the only shutout by the Seahawks in the series (the Raiders got theirs in 1992, when they blanked Seattle 19–0). It also started Seattle's run of six wins in seven games against the Raiders.

Led by Bo Jackson, the Raiders ended that streak impressively on a Monday night in November 1987. It was Bo vs. Boz at the Kingdome, and Jackson and the Raiders won by a knockout, 37–14. Jackson ran for 221 yards, scoring on a 91-yard gallop into one of the Kingdome tunnels and on a two-yard rush on which he carried Bosworth into the end zone.

Nash remembers both plays. During the 91-yard dash, Nash said, "I'm still at the 30-yard line running as fast as I can when he's in the tunnel. He hit that corner as fast as possible and was gone."

As for the infamous Bo vs. Boz play, Nash said Bosworth takes entirely too much heat for that.

"Everyone always talks about the Bosworth showdown," Nash said. "He did get run over, but it was not all due to him. There was a lot of space around him, and the running back had more options, more places to go. If Boz had tried to blow him up, he might have whiffed and been even more embarrassed."

The Seahawks took two from the Raiders in 1988 as Krieg played some of his best football ever, throwing nine touchdown passes. In another Monday night game in November, Krieg threw five touchdown passes and Curt Warner and John L. Williams each ran for more than 100 yards as Seattle won 35–27. Three weeks later, in the season finale, Krieg threw for 410 yards and four touchdowns as the Seahawks won 43–37 to clinch the first AFC West title in franchise history.

The Seahawks finished the series in style on Sunday night, November 11, 2001, when Shaun Alexander set a franchise record with 266 rushing yards in a 34–27 win at Husky Stadium.

Chiefs Weren't Always in Charge

Krieg's touchdown pass to Skansi to win in Kansas City stands as the Seahawks' best win over the Chiefs, but there were some other very notable games in that series.

In their first playoff season, 1983, the Seahawks won a wild 51–48 overtime affair that set a league record for total points scored. Then, the next season, the Seahawks picked the Chiefs apart, winning 45–0 thanks to an NFL-record four interceptions returned for touchdowns.

Seahawks tight end Christian Fauria runs ahead of Kansas City's Donnie Edwards during the third quarter of a critical Seattle win late in 1999 that sealed just their second-ever division title.

In the final game of the 1987 season, the Chiefs poured it on in a 41–20 win that caused the Seahawks to have to go on the road for a wild-card game the next week. But the Seahawks took something positive from the loss, as Largent became the NFL's all-time leading receiver with 751 catches, breaking Charlie Joiner's record of 750.

After Krieg's miracle in Kansas City in 1990, the Seahawks had a major drought against the Chiefs, losing 14 of the next 15 meetings in an ugly stretch that spanned three coaches (Chuck Knox, Tom Flores, and Dennis Erickson).

The last loss in that eight-year dry spell was, appropriately, a very wet one. In Kansas City in 1998, a torrential downpour had water cascading down the stairs of Arrowhead Stadium and into the hallways leading to the locker rooms. The game was suspended briefly, but the rain finally stopped in time for the Chiefs to finish beating the Seahawks 17–6. They also beat up quarterback Warren Moon, who was lost to broken ribs. That was the beginning of Jon Kitna's run as the team's quarterback.

The Seahawks went on to win the next three games in the series, including an important late-season contest in 1999 as the Seahawks fought to pull out of a losing skid and win the AFC West for just the second time ever.

Kicking Butt

The Seahawks always enjoyed their games against the Chargers in the 1980s. And it's no wonder: they went 11–2 against the Chargers from 1983 to 1989, including season sweeps in 1984, 1985, 1986, 1987, and 1989.

Under Don "Air" Coryell, Dan Fouts threw the ball all over the field—to Charlie Joiner, Kellen Winslow, and company. But the Chargers never had any defense. In a seven-game winning streak from 1984 through 1987, the Seahawks averaged 33 points per game and never scored fewer than 24.

Largent loved the Chargers' pass-happy offense—not surprising since he was a receiver—and he enjoyed some of his biggest moments against the Chargers. On the national stage of *Monday Night Football* on October 6, 1986, he set an NFL record by catching a pass in his 128th consecutive game. The Seahawks destroyed San Diego 33–7 that night.

The only game the Chargers won from 1984 to 1989 came in Week 3 of the 1988 season, when they knocked Krieg out of a 17–6 victory at Jack Murphy Stadium. But Largent set the NFL record for career receiving yards (12,167), breaking the old mark (12,146) held by the Chargers' Joiner.

In the early 1990s the ball bounced the other way as the Chargers won nine out of 10 games from 1991 to 1996. But then Seattle won nine out of the last 11 in the AFC West series.

The games between Mike Holmgren's Seahawks and Mike Riley's Chargers always came down to the wire. In 1999 the Chargers swept the Seahawks with two three-point wins: a 13–10 decision in San Diego on John Carney's 41-yard field goal with no time left and a 19–16 victory at the Kingdome in which Seattle's Todd Peterson missed three field goals in the fourth quarter.

But the Seahawks won the last four—with the final three coming courtesy of Rian Lindell's foot. In November 2000 it was

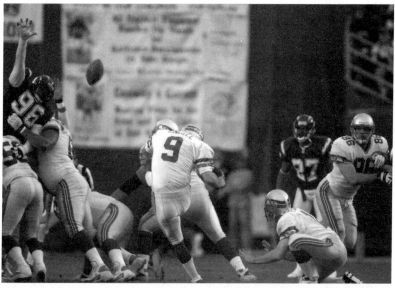

Rian Lindell hits a 54-yard field goal as time runs out to give the Seahawks a 25–22 victory over the Chargers on December 30, 2001, in San Diego.

a 48-yard kick through wind and rain in San Diego with no time left. In December 2001 it was an overtime winner and another last-play pick-me-up.

Lindell added a fourth game-winner against the Chargers in 2002, the Seahawks' first season in the NFC West. It was a fitting reminder of how things had gone in the AFC West.

Butting Heads with the Rams

Mike Holmgren knew exactly what to expect when the Seahawks went from one wild, wild West to another in 2002.

Instead of futilely butting heads with the Denver Broncos, Kansas City Chiefs, Oakland Raiders, and San Diego Chargers—most of whom had dominated the Seahawks for 25 years in the AFC West—the Seahawks would be chasing the St. Louis Rams in the high-scoring NFC West.

"It's a throw-'em-up, scoring division, so we'll have to deal with that," Coach Holmgren told reporters after a minicamp in May 2002.

The Rams possessed the most prolific offense in the NFL—a high-scoring aerial attack that had been dubbed "The Greatest Show on Turf" because of the crowd-pleasing big plays produced by quarterback Kurt Warner, running back Marshall Faulk, and receivers Isaac Bruce and Torry Holt. That quartet and its supporting cast had set NFL records for offense and scoring over the past three seasons, and Warner had been named the most valuable player of the NFL in 1999 and 2001, with Faulk taking the honor in between.

In 2002 the Rams were coming off a 14–2 season and an upset loss to the Patriots in the Super Bowl. But they were the team to beat not only in the NFC West but also in the NFL. At that point, the division title was just a twinkle in the eye of the Seahawks, who were coming off a 9–7 record and second-place finish in their final season in the AFC West.

Although the San Francisco 49ers won the remade NFC West in 2002, they fast faded out of the picture, and the Seahawks and Rams quickly created one of the most exciting young rivalries in the NFL.

RAMS SERIES

- **October 20, 2002:** At Rams 37, Seahawks 20: Marshall Faulk runs for 183 yards and four touchdowns and the Rams batter Seattle quarterback Trent Dilfer into three turnovers and X-rays after the game.
- **December 22, 2002:** At Seahawks 30, Rams 10: Matt Hasselbeck throws for 303 yards and a touchdown, and the Seahawks hold the Rams to 17 rushing yards and knock quarterback Marc Bulger from the game on the fourth play.
- **September 21, 2003:** At Seahawks 24, Rams 23: Shaun Alexander misses the first quarter while attending his daughter's birth, and Matt Hasselbeck throws two fourth-quarter touchdown passes to rally the Seahawks from a 23–10 deficit.
- **December 14, 2003:** At Rams 27, Seahawks 22: A referee accidentally foils Bobby Engram's attempt to catch the winning touchdown pass, tripping the receiver in the final minute, and the Rams clinch the division title.
- **October 10, 2004:** Rams 33, at Seahawks 27, OT: The Rams rally from a 17-point deficit in the final eight minutes of regulation and win on Marc Bulger's 52-yard touchdown pass to Shaun McDonald in overtime.
- **November 14, 2004:** At Rams 23, Seahawks 12: The Rams roll to a 17–0 lead and tie the mistake-prone Seahawks atop the NFC West at 5–4.
- **January 8, 2005:** Rams 27, at Seahawks 20: Marc Bulger throws for 313 yards and two scores, including the winning touchdown with 2:11 left, and the Seahawks' Bobby Engram can't haul in a tough catch in the end zone on fourth down with less than 30 seconds left. The loss knocks the Seahawks out of the first round of the playoffs for the second straight season.
- **October 9, 2005:** Seahawks 37, at Rams 31: Matt Hasselbeck, Shaun Alexander, and Joe Jurevicius lead the Hawks to their first win in St. Louis since they joined the NFC West.
- **November 13, 2005:** At Seahawks 31, Rams 16: Shaun Alexander runs for 165 yards and three touchdowns as the Seahawks win a fifth straight game and take a three-game lead on the Rams in the division.

- **October 15, 2006:** Seahawks 30, at Rams 28: Josh Brown kicks a 54-yard field goal with no time left to lift the Seahawks to their third straight win over the Rams.
- **November 12, 2006:** At Seahawks 24, Rams 22: Josh Brown boots a 38-yard field goal with nine seconds left as the Seahawks beat the Rams for a fourth straight time, despite playing without the injured Matt Hasselbeck and Shaun Alexander.

As Holmgren foreshadowed in 2002, every game in the series has been a high-scoring affair, with an average of 50 points per game and seven of the 11 games, including a playoff contest, decided by seven points or less.

It took three years for the Seahawks to overtake the Rams as division champs, but Seattle kept the title of best in the West for three straight years from 2004 through 2006.

The drama and emotion have been palpable in many of these meetings. The Seahawks have lost three in agonizing fashion and won three in the final minute. They have won a game their starting running back did not start because he was at the hospital for the birth of his first daughter. They have lost one because an official got in the way of a receiver on the potential winning touchdown pass. They have lost one because they blew a 17-point lead in the final six minutes. They have lost a playoff game because they couldn't complete a fourth-down touchdown pass in the final minute. They have won two on the foot of kicker Josh Brown in the final seconds.

The tone was set in 2002 when each team blew out the other while battering its quarterback. And then things got interesting.

On September 21, 2003, Matt Hasselbeck threw two fourth-quarter touchdown passes to rally the Seahawks to a 24–23 win in Seattle. That game was most notable, however, for the fact that running back Shaun Alexander missed the first quarter while attending the birth of his first daughter. He then sped to the stadium behind a police escort and was on the sideline by the start of the second quarter. He immediately lifted his team with runs of 12 and 17 yards. He didn't do much else that day,

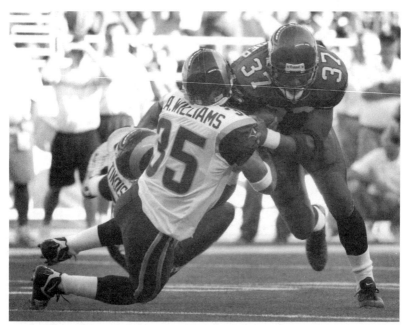

Shaun Alexander bowls over the St. Louis Rams' Aeneas Williams in a
September 21, 2003, game in Seattle. Jackson missed the first quarter to be
with his wife during her delivery of their daughter, then raced to the
stadium to help rally his team past their new rivals.

finishing with just 58 rushing yards, but he and the Seahawks
were ecstatic after Hasselbeck rallied them with touchdown
throws to Darrell Jackson and Koren Robinson—the latter
coming with one minute left.

"Coach Holmgren said, 'We'll win the game when you get
here,' and that was the attitude everyone had," Alexander told
reporters of his delayed arrival. "It made everything go smooth."

As uplifting as that victory was, the game in St. Louis that
season was just the opposite—literally a downer. It ended with
back judge Greg Steed accidentally tripping Bobby Engram as the
receiver prepared to try to catch the winning touchdown pass in
the end zone in the final minute. The Rams escaped with a 27–22
victory and the NFC West title on that December day.

As deflating as that 2003 loss was, nothing beats the contest
on October 10, 2004. The Seahawks finally seemed to have put

themselves in position to challenge the Rams for the division title, and they dominated Mike Martz's team for three and a half quarters, leading 27–10 with less than six minutes left. And then it came crashing down as the Rams rallied to tie the score and then win it in overtime.

Robinson summed up the shocked feelings of the Seahawks and their fans when he told reporters, "It feels like we just lost two games."

It didn't get any better that season, as the Rams dominated the Seahawks 23–12 in St. Louis and then held off Seattle 27–20 in the first round of the playoffs. This latter loss was thanks to a late touchdown pass from Marc Bulger to Cam Cleeland and the Seahawks' inability to score on fourth down from the Rams 4-yard line in the final 30 seconds. Engram once again was Hasselbeck's target on the final pass, which was low and a bit behind the receiver. And the Seahawks were knocked out of the playoffs in the first round for the second straight season.

But the Rams' dominance—five wins in the first seven meetings between the new division rivals—came to an abrupt and unexpected end on October 9, 2005. The Seahawks had not won in St. Louis since 1997, and they were without their top two receivers in a game that Seattle did not seem to have a prayer of winning. But Hasselbeck, Alexander, and Joe Jurevicius did not let that stop them. The quarterback threw for 316 yards and two touchdowns, the running back ran for 119 yards and two scores, and the number three receiver had a career day with nine catches for 137 yards and a touchdown as the Seahawks knocked off the Rams 37–31.

It was a poignant day for Jurevicius, whose play was inspired by thoughts of his late infant son, Michael, who had died in a St. Louis hospital in 2002. The Seahawks had driven past the place on the way to Edward Jones Dome, and the memories and emotions had flooded over the 30-year-old veteran.

"This is a hard place for me to play," the receiver told reporters after the best game of his career. "On my touchdown, I wrote a little M in the grass and threw the ball up to him. So psychologically, I've been through worse, but it's rewarding."

That emotionally charged win was the first of four straight by the Seahawks over the former NFC West champs, with both of the games in 2006 decided in the final seconds by Josh Brown's field goals. He nailed a 54-yarder with no time left on October 15 to lift Seattle to a 30–28 win, and he hit from 38 yards with nine seconds remaining as the Seahawks won 24–22 on November 12 without Hasselbeck and Alexander, who were both injured.

THE PACKERS REUNION TOUR

When Mike Holmgren found out he was going back to Green Bay in his first season as coach of the Seahawks, he wasn't exactly thrilled. Truth be told, he was not happy at all. But the NFL wasn't about to pass up a chance to have the Super Bowl coach return to the city that had named a street after him and face his former team with his new one.

Little did anyone know just how often Holmgren's old and new teams would cross paths, just how many times the coach would have to watch his old student, three-time NFL MVP quarterback Brett Favre, try to carve up Holmgren's new club. It was truly a made-for-TV rivalry.

When Holmgren arrived with so many of his old Packers cronies in 1999, Seattle became Green Bay West. Then the coach, general manager, and executive vice president of the Seahawks, Holmgren brought with him 11 assistant coaches and executives from Green Bay. That didn't include Holmgren's dear friend and defensive wizard, Fritz Shurmur, who died of cancer before he ever could coach a game with the Seahawks.

The Green Bay rivalry only grew when the Seahawks traded Ahman Green to the Packers in 2000 and then obtained Matt Hasselbeck from them in 2001. Every meeting from then on became one giant reunion. The first one, in Green Bay on a Monday night in November 1999, was the first of five contests between Holmgren's two clubs through the 2006 season. The Seahawks' 27–7 victory was the only game the teams played until they met again in 2003, but when realignment came along in

2002 and the Seahawks moved into the same conference as the Packers, it opened the door for many more.

In that first game in 1999, the Seahawks played an inspired contest for their new coach, forcing six turnovers and handing the Packers just their second loss in the past 35 games at legendary Lambeau Field. Ricky Watters ran for 125 yards on 31 carries and told reporters afterward: "We obviously did it for our coach. He came in here with an attitude and a way of doing things that make you proud to be a Seahawk."

Holmgren claimed not to have any secret to stopping his protégé, but Favre threw four interceptions in a game for the first time in five seasons. That helped the Seahawks improve to 5–2 almost midway through a season in which they would eventually claim just their second AFC West title.

The Packers were uncharacteristically undisciplined against their former coach. They committed 10 penalties for 103 yards, including three unsportsmanlike penalties. One of the flags came after Shawn Springs returned a blocked field goal for a touchdown.

PACKERS SERIES

- **November 1, 1999:** Seahawks 27, at Packers 7: In Mike Holmgren's return to Green Bay, Brett Favre turns the ball over six times.
- **October 5, 2003:** At Packers 35, Seahawks 13: Brett Favre throws for two touchdowns and former Seahawk Ahman Green runs for two.
- **January 4, 2004:** At Packers 33, Seahawks 27, OT: Al Harris returns an interception 52 yards for a touchdown in overtime.
- **January 1, 2006:** At Packers 23, Seahawks 17: A coronation for Shaun Alexander, who sets an NFL record with his 28th touchdown, and a celebration of Brett Favre, who leads the Pack past the Hawks backups in a regular-season finale that many speculated was Favre's final game.
- **November 27, 2006:** At Seahawks 34, Packers 24: Matt Hasselbeck returns from a knee injury and Shaun Alexander runs for 201 yards on a team-record 40 carries.

While he celebrated on his way into the end zone, a then-unknown backup quarterback who served as the Packers' holder on field goals arrived to show his displeasure at Springs's gloating. The shove earned the young player a 15-yard penalty, and Seahawks fans had their first glimpse of their fiery future quarterback, a fellow by the name of Matt Hasselbeck.

Hasselbeck's first game against his original team was a dismal defeat, as Favre and Green each accounted for two touchdowns in a 35–13 blowout at Lambeau Field in October 2003. They saw each other again that season in a wild-card playoff game that turned into an overtime shootout in Green Bay. When the Seahawks had won the overtime coin toss, Hasselbeck offered up some playful bravado to Favre and his old Packers friends who had gathered for the coin flip. Not knowing the official's microphone would broadcast his declaration to a national television audience, Hasselbeck proclaimed to his former teammates, "We want the ball, and we're gonna score." It was his bad luck that Green Bay cornerback Al Harris intercepted one of his passes and returned it 52 yards for the winning score.

The games in 2005 and 2006 belonged to Shaun Alexander and Favre. In the 2005 season finale in Green Bay, Alexander set an NFL record with his 28th touchdown of the season and claimed the league rushing title, while Favre played amid advancing speculation that it was the final contest of his Hall of Fame career.

"It was so surreal, like the game didn't even matter," Alexander said a day after the Packers' 23–17 victory. "We were trying to get me a touchdown, and the fans were saying goodbye to Brett."

Favre then seemed to be saying goodbye to Holmgren when he showed up on the Seahawks' plane as the team waited to fly back to Seattle. In fact, Holmgren later said the quarterback told him he had just played his final game. But, over the next three months, Favre changed his mind and decided to return for the 2006 season.

Thus, the 37-year-old quarterback and the Packers made their first trip to Seattle to play Holmgren's club. On that Monday night in late November, Qwest Field more resembled Lambeau as the teams played the first half in a snowstorm. In addition to the usual subplots, the game featured the return of Hasselbeck from a knee injury that had cost him four games, and Alexander had another monumental game, rushing for 201 yards on a team-record 40 carries in the Seahawks' 34–24 win.

Mike Holmgren embraces Green Bay Packers quarterback Brett Favre after their game on January 1, 2006, in Green Bay.

BATTLES WITH THE BENGALS

Perhaps not many would consider it a rivalry, but for most of a decade, the Seahawks and Cincinnati Bengals were almost like division rivals.

Through the 2006 season, the Seahawks had played as many games against Cincinnati (16) as they had against current division opponents San Francisco and Arizona. In fact, the Seahawks and Bengals met every year from 1984 to 1995, with the Seahawks winning seven of those 12 games. The teams were 8–8 overall in those 16 meetings.

The contests in the late 1980s were some of the most entertaining games the Seahawks played at that time: the 1988 playoff game that featured Joe "Trick Knee" Nash; the late-season game in 1989 in which Steve Largent caught his record-setting 100th touchdown and Cincinnati coach Sam Wyche had some sharp words for the home fans; and the 1990 game in which Rufus Porter became a man possessed.

The 1988 season was the only one in the 12-year stretch in which the teams were not scheduled to meet. But, as luck would have it, they met up in the playoffs anyway. Both teams had won their divisions, the Seahawks for the first time after beating the Los Angeles Raiders in the season finale to finish 9–7.

The Bengals had turned from a 4–11 team in 1987 to a 12–4 winner of the AFC Central in 1988 thanks to Wyche's inventive offense. They were led by quarterback Boomer Esiason, the blond bomber who was the NFL's MVP, and rookie running back Ickey "Shuffle" Woods. Esiason was the maestro of Wyche's no-huddle offense, a newfangled scheme that had caused teams headaches all season and enabled the Bengals to lead the league in scoring (448 points). The scheme was about controlling tempo, with the offensive players not huddling up in the usual fashion but gathering around the line of scrimmage in what they called the Sugar Huddle. It prevented defenses from substituting players because the Bengals would quickly snap the ball to create a penalty against the defense for illegal substitution.

Steve Largent receives his 100th career touchdown pass against the
Cincinnati Bengals at Riverfront Stadium on December 10, 1989. This grab
broke the 44-year-old record for touchdown catches that was previously
held by Don Hutson.

The Seahawks knew all about the trouble the Bengals were
causing defenses, and they came up with a way to slow it down.
His name was Joe "Trick Knee" Nash.

When the Seahawks needed to give themselves time to substitute players, Coach Knox would signal for a player to go down
with an "injury." One arm raised meant the nose tackle was the
actor, two arms meant the defensive end would fake it.

As it turned out, Nash was "hurt" four times in that game.

"We'd look over to the sideline to Chuck, and every time it was
Joe," linebacker Dave Wyman said of the coach's one-armed signal.

"Rumor has it Chuck forgot the signals and would just do the
one," Nash said.

It was ironic that Nash was the guy who ended up taking the
fall most of the afternoon. This was a guy who, as Wyman said,

"just despised guys who laid on the field," and then Nash went on to become the Seahawks' all-time iron man, with a club-record 218 games played.

Nash regrets that among all of his accomplishments—most games played, a Pro Bowl in 1984, a team-record 10 blocked kicks (eight on field goals)—he is often best remembered for his "trick knee."

"I played for 15 years, and unfortunately that's what some people remember out of my 15 years," he said. "It was something that as a team you have to do something. What do you do?"

Nash pulled up lame four times, and when he wasn't in the game it was backup nose tackle Ken Clarke. The Bengals became annoyed at the Seahawks' slowdown tactic.

Esiason told referee Red Cashion, "Come on, Red. If this guy goes down with the same injury, you would think he was missing ligaments or a kneecap by now."

At the time, Wyche begrudgingly gave the Seahawks credit for the ploy, telling reporters, "Smart coaching by the Seahawks. We complained about it, but we've had people complain about the no-huddle."

All of the drama and nose dives by nose tackles didn't help much. The Bengals ran for 254 yards and three touchdowns—two by Stanley Wilson and one by Woods, who rushed for 126 yards—and beat the Seahawks 21–13.

In the end, all the Seahawks had to show for the playoff game was one of the more innovative defensive strategies in playoff history as pulled off by one of the Seahawks' all-time tough guys.

"That's how tough Joe was," Dave Krieg quipped. "He kept getting up and going back in there. Gutsy game by Joe."

Largent and Wyche on Their Toes

The Bengals and Seahawks met again late in the 1989 season. The Seahawks were 5–8 and long shots to make the playoffs after going 0–4 in November, and the Bengals were 7–6 and on their way to 8–8. It wasn't as high stakes as the last meeting, but the game had plenty of drama.

The first act came with 42 seconds left in first half, when Largent caught his 100th touchdown to pass Don Hutson (99) for the NFL record. Krieg couldn't find his primary target and was about to pull the ball down when he saw Largent alone in the back of the end zone. The future Hall of Famer, who already had set most of the league's career receiving records, had to reach high for the ball, and he came down on his tiptoes before falling out of the back of the end zone.

The Seahawks didn't pull out ol' Trick Knee Nash, but they were called for 12 men on the field twice in the second half when they tried to make third-down substitutions. Then the Hawks came up with a new way of giving themselves time to substitute. As the teams lined up for another third down in the fourth quarter, Wyman "accidentally" kicked the ball, giving teammates time to shuttle on and off the field.

In the fourth quarter, the Seahawks were witness to one of the oddest scenes ever at an NFL game. With 10 minutes left, the Seahawks led 17–10 and were backed up almost to their end zone, and Bengals fans began to pelt them with snowballs. It was the kind of ill-mannered behavior that had been popularized by fans in Cleveland's Dawg Pound and that Bengals owner Paul Brown had complained about earlier that year.

While the officials tried to get security to handle it, Wyche intervened. After consulting the referees, he ran across the field, grabbed a microphone, and told the crowd, "Will the next person that sees anybody throw anything on this field, point 'em out and get 'em out of here?" Then he drew a huge cheer when he added, "You don't live in Cleveland; you live in Cincinnati!"

The Seahawks ended up winning a very good game, 24–17, but the result was a mere aside to Largent's NFL record and Wyche's mid-game insult toward Cleveland fans.

Raise the Rufe!

As if the Bengals-Seahawks series hadn't been dramatic enough over the past two years, the Monday night game in October 1990 raised the bar another level.

It was billed as a monstrous mismatch because the Bengals were 3–0 and the Seahawks were 0–3. But Seattle's defense shut down Cincinnati's high-powered attack and the Seahawks came away with a 31–16 victory at the Kingdome. One man determined the direction of the game.

It all started when Rufus Porter slammed Esiason to the turf on a play that had been blown dead. Porter had not heard the whistle in the raucous Kingdome. Esiason and Porter exchanged blows, and Porter was lucky he was not ejected. But the penalty just fired Porter up.

"Rufus would not step down from anybody," Nash said. "He was not a big guy, and wasn't real intense. But once he got going, he was hard to stop."

On the next play, Porter batted down one of Esiason's passes and pointed tauntingly in Esiason's face. That incited the crowd of 60,135 even more, with chants of "Rufe, Rufe, Rufe" echoing around the deafening Dome. That caused the Bengals to commit a delay of game.

Then, with the crowd even louder, Porter knocked down another pass by Esiason. He induced left tackle Anthony Munoz into multiple false starts while also getting by the future Hall of Famer for two sacks.

"He could come around the corner like no one I'd ever seen," Wyman said of Porter, who had 35 sacks from 1989 to 1992. "He was like a jet plane how he could angle and bank."

NUMBERS DON'T LIE [OR DO THEY?]

THESE GUYS DESERVED BETTER

Fullback is perhaps the most overlooked position in football. It was so overlooked in the NFL that the league didn't create a Pro Bowl spot for the position until 1993.

If it had, John L. Williams would have gone to the all-star game more than the two times he was chosen. And if Tampa Bay's Mike Alstott hadn't been a halfback masquerading as a fullback, Mack Strong would have been in the Pro Bowl long before his first trip in 2005.

Williams and Strong came from opposite ends of the talent pool—Williams was a first-round pick in 1986 and Strong was an undrafted free agent in 1993. But they were both among the most underrated players in the league for most of their careers, even though their contributions to the success of their teams are quite apparent.

Williams was more than just a blocking fullback. He was a capable runner, a great blocker, and one of the best receiving backs in NFL history. His huge, soft hands hauled in 471 passes over eight seasons—the third most in franchise history. He had six seasons with 50 or more catches—second in team history to Steve Largent's 10 such seasons.

Dave Krieg, who played with Williams from 1986 to 1991 and threw most of those 471 passes to him, said the fullback was "very underrated."

"He was very smart. Great football sense. Great hands, great blocker, great teammate."

In Williams's rookie season, Curt Warner set a team record with 1,481 rushing yards and scored 13 touchdowns. And he accomplished much of it behind Williams, who added 538 rushing yards himself.

In 1988 Warner ran for 1,025 yards while Williams added 877 rushing yards and caught a team-high 58 passes. With 1,528 total yards and seven touchdowns, Williams should have made the Pro Bowl ahead of New England's John Stephens (1,168 yards).

Williams finally did make it onto the all-star team in 1990, when he caught 73 passes and combined for 1,413 yards. He was voted on again in 1991, when he caught 61 balls and tallied 1,240 yards.

Strong had an even longer wait for recognition. He rode the pine on the practice squad during his first season, but he turned himself into a classic blocking fullback and helped pave the way for 1,000-yard rushers in 10 of his first 12 seasons. He was the main fullback for six straight 1,000-yard rushing seasons from 2000 through 2005, including Shaun Alexander's league-leading 1,880 yards in 2005.

Although Strong should have been to the Pro Bowl as early as 2001 and certainly in both 2003 and 2004—when Alexander tallied 3,131 yards and scored 30 touchdowns—Strong finally was recognized as the NFC's best fullback in 2005. He also was picked in 2006, which was more a product of his belated reputation as one of the best.

It was a testament to Strong's perseverance, because in order to get those honors, he had to hold off three fullbacks the team drafted to try to replace him—from Reggie Brown (1996) to Heath Evans (2001) to Chris Davis (2003). The Seahawks spent two third-round picks and a fifth-rounder on those guys, yet Strong outlasted them all.

"We drafted, in the last few years, a couple guys to kind of replace Mack because at some point everyone's career ends," Coach Holmgren said in January 2006. "But, I'll be darned, we can't do it. This year, I think he was about as good as you can be at that position, and he was rewarded with the Pro Bowl."

John L. Williams (left) and Mack Strong were two of the most underrated players in the league during their careers.

Williams photo courtesy of Getty Images.

PUTTIN' IN THEIR TIME

Three of the top six Seahawks in games played were not even drafted (Joe Nash, Mack Strong, and Eugene Robinson). Following are the top 20 most-tenured Seahawks.

Player	Seasons	Games
Joe Nash	15 (1982–96)	218
Steve Largent	14 (1976–89)	200
Mack Strong	14 (1994–Present)	196
Jacob Green	12 (1980–91)	178
Jeff Bryant	12 (1982–93)	175
Eugene Robinson	11 (1985–95)	170
Cortez Kennedy	11 (1990–2000)	167
Dave Brown	11 (1976–86)	159
Brian Blades	11 (1988–98)	156
Walter Jones	10 (1997–Present)	154
Keith Butler	10 (1978–87)	146
Michael Sinclair	11 (1991–2001)	144
Chris Gray	9 (1998–2006)	142
Edwin Bailey	11 (1981–91)	139
Norm Johnson	9 (1982–90)	134
Mike Tice	10 (1981–88, 1990–91)	130
Dave Krieg	12 (1980–91)	129
Chris Warren	8 (1990–97)	123
John L. Williams	8 (1986–93)	123
Bryan Millard	8 (1984–91)	121

Through 2006 Strong had played in 196 games over 14 seasons, making him the number three most-tenured Seahawk behind Joe Nash (218 games) and Steve Largent (200). And, like Largent, the fullback's contributions have not been limited to the field. In fact, his teammates voted him a four-time winner of the Steve Largent Award—given to the player who best exemplifies the spirit, dedication, and integrity of the Seahawks. Since the award was created in 1989, no one else had won it more than once.

Strong made a believer out of Holmgren, who said during the 2005 season, "Mack Strong is about my favorite player of all time. The Mack Strongs of the world make it worth my while to coach and teach. He is unselfish. He has played 13 years, longer than anybody we have. He does all the dirty work. He is the lead blocker most every play for our halfback. He is a great man in the community. He is a great father and a wonderful family guy.... I can't say enough about him."

A Long Line of Pro Bowl Snubs

A quarterback from another team once said to Krieg, "You played 10 years in Seattle and never had a Pro Bowl lineman?"

It was true. From 1983 to 1988, the Seahawks went to the playoffs four times and put 24 players in the Pro Bowl, but none of them was an offensive lineman.

"They all did a great job. They just didn't get the recognition," Krieg said.

The ones who deserved it most were the interior three. Center Blair Bush was signed before the 1983 season and proceeded to anchor the middle as the Seahawks scored a team-record 50 touchdowns and 403 points. Bush also led a quintet that paved the way for rookie Curt Warner to rush for a team-record 1,449 yards.

In 1984 Edwin Bailey took over full time for aging left guard Reggie McKenzie and was part of a line that helped Krieg throw for team records of 3,671 yards and 32 touchdowns after Warner was hurt in the opener. The team went 12–4 that season and sent a team-record seven players to the Pro Bowl. But none of them was an offensive lineman.

"We really should have had a lineman in the Pro Bowl in 1984," Krieg lamented of a line that included Bush, Bailey, Ron Essink, Robert Pratt, and Bob Cryder.

Unbelievably, the Seahawks went through their first 23 seasons without a Pro Bowl lineman. Until Walter Jones was named to the all-star unit in 1999, the best honor accorded a Seattle lineman had been when right guard Bryan Millard was chosen as an All-Pro by NFL Films in 1987 and by *Sports Illustrated*

Walter Jones, the franchise's first Pro Bowl offensive lineman in 1999, protects quarterback Matt Hasselbeck in a 2005 game.

in 1988. Before Steve Hutchinson joined Jones as the second Seattle lineman to make the Pro Bowl, Millard had been widely considered the best guard in team history. He and Bailey started together from 1986 to 1990 and were the best tandem until Hutchinson and Chris Gray manned the guard spots from 2001 through 2005.

Gray joined the Seahawks as a free agent in 1998 and proceeded to ever so quietly set a franchise record by starting 121 consecutive games. His run ended when a bruised quadriceps kept him out of the 2006 season finale in Tampa Bay.

Center Robbie Tobeck had been similarly unnoticed throughout his first five seasons with the team, but he joined Jones and Hutchinson in the Pro Bowl after helping Shaun Alexander win the MVP during the Seahawks' Super Bowl run in 2005. And with that, the Seahawks had gone from extremely under-recognized along the line to very well represented in Hawaii.

Butler Did It

How underrated was Keith Butler? He never made the Pro Bowl even though he was worth two first-round draft picks.

That's what the Seahawks got in exchange for Fredd Young when they sent him to Indianapolis in 1988. And Butler was the one who helped make Young so valuable while he played for the Seahawks.

No one disputes that Young was a playmaker extraordinaire. The guy made the Pro Bowl in all four of his seasons in Seattle—the first two as a special-teams standout and the next two as a starting linebacker. Young led the Seahawks in tackles every year from 1985 to 1987, recording 18 sacks (he also caused five fumbles and recovered four in 1987). He was the Seahawks' Lawrence Taylor Light.

But he was able to do it all because Butler was right beside him as the other inside linebacker in the Seahawks' 3–4 defense. And because defensive coordinator Tom Catlin allowed Young to do it.

"Fredd owed part of his salary to Keith Butler," nose tackle Joe Nash cracked. "Fredd was an unbelievable talent; he could fly. But a lot of times he would decide to rush the passer when he should have been covering and vice versa. And Keith would cover for him."

Nash said there were times when Young was supposed to cover the right side of the field and Butler was assigned to the left, and Young would decide to go after the quarterback, so Butler would simply cover the entire middle of the field.

Quarterback Dave Krieg said the arrangement worked because the two inside linebackers complemented one another.

"Keith Butler was a very smart linebacker and had to use his smarts," Krieg said. "Freddie Young had athleticism and could use instincts. If he saw something, he would go by gut instinct and freelance a bit. Butler made up for it with football instincts and playbook knowledge."

The importance of Butler's influence on Young became quite apparent when Young failed to make much impact with the Colts after he was traded in 1988. He lasted just three seasons in Indy and then was out of football.

Butler, Seattle's second-round pick in 1978, became one of the best Seahawks of all time—he started 132 games over 10 years and is the number two tackler in franchise history (813). But he never got as much credit as he deserved.

STARTING STREAKS

Unsung guard Chris Gray passed Cortez Kennedy for the team record for consecutive starts in 2005, and the streak came to an end when a bruised quadriceps held Gray out of the 2006 season finale in Tampa Bay. The Seahawks' four iron men:

Player	Consecutive starts (Years)
Chris Gray	121 (1998–2006)
Cortez Kennedy	100 (1990–97)
Jacob Green	92 (1980–87)
Eugene Robinson	92 (1985–94)

Not Even a Sniff of the Hall

Only six men in NFL history intercepted more passes than the late Dave Brown, who finished his 16-year career with 62 picks, which is more than 13 of the 17 defensive backs in the Pro Football Hall of Fame. Yet Brown has long been overlooked by the 40 sportswriters who have the honor of immortalizing players in the Hall.

"He had 62 interceptions, and he doesn't get a sniff of the Hall of Fame? How's that possible?" wondered Paul Moyer, who played alongside Brown for four seasons and coached the Seahawks' secondary with him for three years.

Obtained from the Pittsburgh Steelers in the 1976 veteran allocation draft, Brown became one of the Seahawks' best defenders over the next decade. He is still the best cornerback to ever play for the team, holding team records in interceptions (50), interceptions for touchdowns (five), and return yards off interceptions (643).

Moyer called Brown a consummate technician and a sure tackler with great hands and a beautiful backpedal.

"He was an absolute playmaker," Moyer said. "It's hard to get that many interceptions playing cornerback."

The only cornerbacks in NFL history with more interceptions are Dick "Night Train" Lane (68) and Ken Riley (65). The four other men with more interceptions played all or much of their careers at safety.

Brown actually started his Seattle career at safety, intercepting four passes from that position in 1976. He then moved over to corner for the rest of his career and was as consistent as cornerbacks come. He started every game in 10 of his 11 seasons and recorded at least four interceptions in eight of those years. But he made the Pro Bowl just once, when he intercepted eight passes in 1984. He returned two of those picks for touchdowns against the Kansas City Chiefs on November 4—part of the Seahawks' NFL-record four interceptions for touchdowns that day.

Brown finished his career in Green Bay, where he played for three seasons and finished with 62 interceptions—tied for seventh in NFL history. He then rejoined the Seahawks in 1992 as a defensive assistant and coached under Tom Flores and Dennis Erickson until Mike Holmgren succeeded Erickson in 1999.

In 2001 Brown was hired on to coach defensive backs at Texas Tech and was still working in that capacity when he shockingly died of an apparent heart attack after collapsing during a pick-up basketball game at the university in Lubbock, Texas, in January 2006. He was 52.

WERE THEY WORTH IT?

In the 1980s the Seahawks were a franchise of seeming overachievers—guys like Steve Largent, Dave Krieg, Joe Nash, Eugene Robinson, and Rufus Porter.

In the 1990s, due to some incredibly terrible drafting, the team was full of underachievers. Along with Brian Bosworth, first-round quarterbacks Kelly Stouffer, Dan McGwire, and Rick Mirer were the biggest busts in franchise history (and thus earned their own chapters in this compilation).

But other than those high-profile guys, the Seahawks haven't had a lot of overrated players. Sure, they graded some guys higher than they should have been in the draft. McGwire was one of the

NFL CAREER INTERCEPTIONS LEADERS

No.	Player	Seasons
81	Paul Krause*	16
79	Emlen Tunnell*	14
71	Rod Woodson	17
68	Dick Lane*	15
65	Ken Riley	15
63	Ronnie Lott*	14
62	Dave Brown	16
62	Dick LeBeau	14

*Hall of Famer

Note: Brown has more interceptions than Hall of Famers Mel Blount (57), Lem Barney (56), Willie Brown (54), Mel Renfro (52), Larry Wilson (52), and Yale Lary (50). Darrell Green had 54, Deion Sanders 53.

biggest examples of that. When they saw him on the practice field, some defensive players couldn't believe McGwire had been drafted at all—let alone in the first round.

A few players have been overrated for other reasons.

Before Shaun Alexander became MVP in 2005, he was widely considered an underachieving runner who tried hard only when he smelled the end zone and who went down too easily so as to spare himself from injury. But his hard running in 2005, when he led the NFL with 1,880 rushing yards, put an end to most of that *overrated* talk.

In St. Louis, Grant Wistrom earned a reputation as one of the best all-around defensive ends in the NFL. But he suddenly became overrated when he became overpaid, getting a franchise-record $14 million signing bonus from Seattle in 2004. He made more than $20 million while playing in just 41 games before he was released in March 2007.

In 1990 the Seahawks used a second-round pick to draft Robert Blackmon, a safety from Baylor's well-respected defense who was expected to step into the void that had not been filled since All-Pro Kenny Easley was forced into early retirement in 1988.

Blackmon proceeded to start 96 games over seven seasons. But he lasted as the starter only because the team didn't have anyone better to put next to Robinson. Blackmon played a lot as a rookie and then started every game in 1991, but he wasn't even among the team's six best tacklers. Even defensive tackle Cortez Kennedy recorded more tackles—a testament to Blackmon's lack of involvement as much as to Kennedy's greatness. In fact, in his seven seasons, Blackmon was among the team's top four tacklers just once.

The coaches kept thinking Blackmon would come around and turn into the thumper he had been at Baylor. But it never happened. Some coaches thought he was too tentative and afraid to make big hits.

In 1998 the Seahawks used their first-round pick on Anthony Simmons, a lightning-fast linebacker from Clemson, and figured to put him on the side opposite Pro Bowl linebacker Chad Brown. Simmons split time with Darrin Smith in his first season and showed flashes of his incredible athletic ability.

In 1999 new coach Mike Holmgren moved him to middle linebacker for lack of better options. The position was not a good fit for a guy who was used to playing in space and using his speed, so Holmgren moved Simmons back outside in 2000. The linebacker responded by leading the team with 147 tackles—the third most in franchise history.

When the Seahawks moved to the NFC West in 2002, they were excited about being able to use the speedy Simmons to cover

ONE RECORD LARGENT DOES NOT HOLD

Although he was one of the original Seahawks, Hall of Famer Steve Largent was not the first Seahawk to record a 100-yard receiving game. That honor went to Sam McCullum, who caught four passes for 112 yards and two touchdowns in Seattle's first game, a 30–24 loss to the St. Louis Cardinals on September 12, 1976.

Marshall Faulk, the St. Louis Rams' multi-threat running back. But a sprained ankle ruined those plans as Simmons missed nine games.

That didn't dissuade the Seahawks, who in 2003 decided Simmons was worth a long-term investment and gave him a five-year deal worth $23.75 million. They expected him to be one of the key cogs in new coordinator Ray Rhodes's aggressive, speed-based defense. But that never happened either because Simmons clashed with linebackers coach John Marshall and couldn't escape injuries.

Thus, after seven largely unfulfilled seasons, Simmons was cut in March 2005.

TRADING PLACES

MORE THAN TRUE VALUE

The second trade the Seahawks ever made still stands as the best trade they ever made. On August 26, 1976, they shipped an eighth-round draft choice to the Houston Oilers for a guy who would turn out to be worth multiple first-round picks as he proceeded to turn into one of the best wide receivers the NFL had ever seen. An eighth-round pick for a Hall of Famer? That's value. And that was how the team got Steve Largent.

The Seahawks have made a few other big-value trades over the years as well. They netted two first-round picks from the Indianapolis Colts for linebacker Fredd Young and turned them into Andy Heck and Cortez Kennedy (see chapter 4). And they obtained quarterback Matt Hasselbeck when they threw in a third-round pick and swapped spots in the first round with Green Bay.

The Seahawks also managed to salvage great value from two former first-round picks who did not fit in the team's plans, Rick Mirer and Joey Galloway.

A Bear Market for Mirer

Mirer, Seattle's first-round pick in 1993, had worn out his welcome by early in the 1996 season. Dennis Erickson had inherited Mirer when he became coach in 1995, and the quarterback was just not a good fit in Erickson's spread offense; Mirer quickly had shown he could not throw the ball downfield with any accuracy.

By early October 1996, the Seahawks were 1–4 and Erickson had benched Mirer for John Friesz. Then the Seahawks began to work on trading the former number two overall draft pick. They had serious discussions with the Atlanta Falcons about trading starting quarterbacks, Mirer for Jeff George, who had been suspended after a sideline altercation with coach June Jones.

That deal never materialized, but the Seahawks did even better after the season, sending Mirer and a fourth-round pick to the Chicago Bears for the Bears' first-round pick in the 1997 draft. It was one of the great fleece jobs in Seahawks history—a deal orchestrated by general manager Randy Mueller, who knew the Bears coveted Mirer enough to surrender the 11th choice in the draft.

DID YOU KNOW...

Seattle's first kicker was not Efren Herrera. John Leypoldt kicked the first two seasons, and the Seahawks obtained Herrera—one of the team's cult heroes—in August 1978 by sending a 1979 fifth-round draft pick to Dallas.

"I'm happy that, for Rick's sake, we were able to send him somewhere he wanted to go and that we were able to get compensated fairly," Mueller told reporters after the deal was consummated on February 18, 1997. "Obviously a big piece to our puzzle is acquiring another first-round pick."

The deal gave the Seahawks the 11th and 12th picks in the draft, which they parlayed into one of the best first rounds in franchise history. In March they sent the 11th pick—along with their second, third, and fourth choices—to Atlanta for the third overall pick and Atlanta's third-rounder. Then, on draft day, the Seahawks sent that third-rounder and their other first-rounder to Tampa Bay for the sixth overall choice. It is the only time in franchise history that the Seahawks have held two picks in the top 10 of the draft. And they turned them into two of the best players in franchise history, taking cornerback Shawn Springs with the third pick and future All-Pro left tackle Walter Jones with the sixth pick.

Chicago coach Dave Wannstedt was happy to get Mirer, telling reporters, "We believe Rick has the qualities to be an outstanding player and help us get to the next level. This trade solidifies our quarterback position. This is an important decision by the organization but one we feel will pay off in the future."

It certainly paid off for the Seahawks. Springs started 88 games during his seven seasons in Seattle and made the Pro Bowl in 1998. Jones merely turned into the best offensive lineman in the NFL, making the Pro Bowl seven times from 1999 through 2006.

Meanwhile, Mirer played in just seven games with the 4–12 Bears in 1997 and was gone after the season. He bounced around to three other teams before his career ended in 2003. And the Bears fired Wannstedt after another 4–12 record in 1998.

Galloway for an MVP

A year-long standoff between Mike Holmgren and Joey Galloway ended on February 12, 2000, when the coach/general manager traded the mercurial receiver to the Dallas Cowboys for two first-round draft picks.

Galloway, Seattle's first-round pick in 1995, had held out for eight months, refusing to sign what he considered a substandard contract. He returned to the team eight games into Holmgren's first season only because he wanted to get credit for the season so he could become an unrestricted free agent. The Seahawks challenged whether he had actually qualified for free agency, but an arbitrator ruled in Galloway's favor, so the team made him its exclusive franchise player, meaning he could not negotiate with any teams without Seattle's permission.

Cowboys owner Jerry Jones was enamored with Galloway's spectacular speed (under 4.2 seconds in the 40-yard dash) and was prepared to pay both the Seahawks and the receiver. Thus, he surrendered first-round picks in 2000 and 2001 to Seattle and paid Galloway a $12.5 million bonus as part of a seven-year, $42 million deal.

"There has been only one other time I have really broken the bank like this in free agency, and that was for [cornerback] Deion [Sanders]," Jones told Dallas reporters. "But earlier this year we made a philosophical change on offense and we decided we needed to go for the jugular, to get a great player, an impact player who can win games for us, and we think Joey is that player."

It never happened. Galloway blew out his knee in his first game with the Cowboys and played three more seasons with a bevy of bad quarterbacks before being traded to Tampa Bay for Keyshawn Johnson.

Meanwhile, the Seahawks used their bonus 2000 first-round pick, the 19th overall, on running back Shaun Alexander. And their 2001 pick, which turned out to be the seventh overall because the Cowboys were so bad in 2000, became wide receiver Koren Robinson. One out of two isn't bad.

While Robinson never lived up to expectations and was cut before the 2005 season after numerous alcohol-related problems, Alexander turned into the best back in Seattle history. He is the franchise's career leader in rushing yards and touchdowns and has steadily carved his place in league annals as well. In 2005 Alexander was named the most valuable player of the NFL while leading the league with 1,880 rushing yards and setting the since-broken league record with 28 touchdowns.

WHY'D THEY DO THAT?

While the Seahawks have had some bad drafts—especially in the 1970s and early 1990s—they have not often made many mistakes in the trading game. They have pulled some major coups, such as getting two first-rounders each for linebacker Fredd Young and wide receiver Joey Galloway and another first-rounder for quarterback Rick Mirer. But there certainly have been a few deals that didn't work out the way the team had hoped.

The biggest trade bust in team history is the one that brought quarterback Kelly Stouffer to Seattle in 1988. The Seahawks originally tried to send safety Kenny Easley to the Phoenix Cardinals for Stouffer, who had sat out his rookie season in a contract dispute. But Easley failed his physical, and the Seahawks ended up giving the Cardinals three draft picks for Stouffer—a fifth-round pick in 1988 and first- and fifth-rounder in 1989.

Kelly Stouffer's tenure in Seattle was far less successful than anticipated. Photo courtesy of Getty Images.

PIT STOPS BY HALL OF FAMERS

Steve Largent is the only career Seahawk in the Hall of Fame, but three other Famers spent time in Seattle at the end of their careers.

Defensive end Carl Eller, 1979

A six-time Pro Bowl player as a member of the Minnesota Vikings' "Purple People Eaters" defensive line, Eller was one of the best all-around ends in the NFL from 1967 to 1973. Sacks were not an official statistic when he played, but Eller recorded 44 quarterback takedowns from 1975 to 1977. He played the final season of his 16-year career in Seattle and was inducted into the Hall of Fame in 2004.

Running back Franco Harris, 1984

The Pittsburgh Steelers' first-round draft pick in 1972, Harris was a nine-time Pro Bowl running back and a member of the Steelers' four Super Bowl teams. He was the MVP of Super Bowl IX—the first of the Steelers' four titles. Harris finished his career with 12,120 yards—good for third all-time when he retired—and 91 touchdowns. He finished his 13-year career by playing in eight games with the Seahawks in 1984. He was inducted into the Hall of Fame in 1990.

Quarterback Warren Moon, 1997–98

Moon joined the franchise in 1997 after having already played six seasons in the Canadian Football League, 10 with the Houston Oilers and three with the Vikings. Moon had gone to eight Pro Bowls as an Oiler and Viking, and he added a ninth Pro Bowl as a Seahawk after setting franchise records with 313 completions and 3,678 yards. Moon started 25 games for the Seahawks. In 23 professional seasons, he threw for more than 70,000 yards and finished third in NFL history in attempts, completions, and yards (he is now ranked fourth in each category). He was inducted into the Hall of Fame in 2006.

"We think he'll be the quarterback of the future," Seahawks general manager Mike McCormack told reporters on April 22, 1988, the day the trade was made and Stouffer was signed to a four-year deal worth about $3 million.

Because of an injury to Dave Krieg, Stouffer ended up starting six games in his first season in Seattle. But he never could unseat Krieg, who remained the starter through 1991. Stouffer started just 16 games in five years with the Seahawks, and he was gone after helping lead one of the worst offenses in NFL history in 1992.

Cornering the Market?

In 2000 the Seahawks were desperate for depth at cornerback, so general manager Mike Holmgren swung another deal with his former team.

The first one had turned out okay—giving up a seventh-round pick to Green Bay in 1999 for receiver Derrick Mayes, who helped the Seahawks reach the playoffs for the first time in 11 seasons.

This deal seemed to make perfect sense—sending a fumble-prone backup running back for a coveted cover corner. But when the corner, Fred Vinson, ended up never playing a down for the Seahawks while the back, Ahman Green, went on to become a four-time Pro Bowl rusher, it turned out to be the worst deal Holmgren made as GM.

The day before the draft in 2000, the Seahawks sent Green and a fifth-round pick to the Packers for Vinson and a sixth-rounder. The Seahawks had grown weary of Green's habit of fumbling, and they didn't really need the former third-round pick because they had Ricky Watters. And, as it turned out, the Seahawks found the immediate replacement for Green and the eventual successor to Watters when Shaun Alexander fell to them at the 19th spot in the first round of the draft.

Vinson, meanwhile, was expected to add depth to a Seattle secondary that had been racked by injuries the previous season. Vinson had been the Packers' second-round pick in 1999—selected with the choice the Seahawks had surrendered for the right to sign Holmgren as their coach and general manager that year. The Seahawks had liked Vinson in that draft, even though he was coming off a foot injury that occurred during his senior year at Vanderbilt.

The injury bothered Vinson throughout his first NFL season, but the Seahawks were not concerned about it and had no qualms surrendering Green, who had been drafted under the Dennis Erickson regime and had not earned Holmgren's trust after fumbling four times in the 1999 preseason.

"They wanted Ahman. We needed a corner," Holmgren told reporters. "This is a good move for us."

Well, it might have been, if not for two knee injuries suffered by Vinson. He blew out the anterior cruciate ligament in his right knee during a minicamp in June 2000 and missed the season. Then he tore the ACL again in April 2001 and never played a down for the Seahawks.

And Holmgren never lived it down after Green went on to rush for over 8,000 yards and 53 touchdowns for Holmgren's old team from 2000 to 2006.

The Dorsett Deal

When the Seahawks traded the number two pick in the 1977 draft, thereby handing the rights to Tony Dorsett to the Dallas Cowboys, Minnesota coach Bud Grant could not believe it.

Grant told reporters the Seahawks and Cowboys "must be sleeping together."

"I don't understand it at all," Grant railed. "Most people felt Dorsett was the premier player in the draft—similar to [O.J.] Simpson several years ago."

Everyone likes to lament the fact that the Seahawks passed on a chance to draft a future Hall of Fame running back, and while Seattle's trade with the Dallas Cowboys looks bad in retrospect, it's hard to say the Seahawks made a mistake. They were a second-year franchise in need of as many players as they could get, and four good players were more useful than one great player.

If they had kept the number two overall pick and selected Dorsett, there's no guarantee the running back would have been able to duplicate the 1,000-yard, rookie-of-the-year season he had in 1977. In Dallas, Dorsett joined an established team that was ready to win the Super Bowl—and did just that.

In Seattle he would have been running behind a cobbled-together line that was still being, well, cobbled together.

Besides, the Seahawks needed more than just a running back. And they got more than just a running back by picking up the 14th overall pick and three second-round choices from Dallas in the blockbuster deal. In order, they drafted offensive lineman Steve August, lineman Tom Lynch, and linebacker Terry Beeson. They traded the third second-round pick back to Dallas for receiver Duke Fergerson.

While Dorsett went on to become one of the best running backs in NFL history, the Seahawks got what they needed out of the players they obtained. Beeson started as a rookie and for four years beyond that, while August and Lynch joined the starting line in 1978. Lynch started 48 games at left guard before being traded to Buffalo in 1981, while August started 90 games at right tackle, including 15 in the 1983 playoff season. Fergerson started eight games in 1977 and was with the Seahawks for three seasons.

Better to Give Than Receive?

If Steve Largent had not turned into a seven-time Pro Bowl player, the Seahawks might have regretted the decision to trade Ahmad Rashad before they had ever played a game. As it is, the Seahawks got what they could for a wide receiver who had not played the previous season and who regretted his decision to sign with the team from the start.

Rashad, who grew up in Tacoma as Bobby Moore, decided to sign with the hometown team in 1976 after missing the 1975 season with a knee injury. But he didn't come back because he was homesick. He signed with Seattle only because the Seahawks offered more money ($125,000) than his former team, the Buffalo Bills ($90,000).

Rashad clashed with coaches throughout camp, and the Seahawks grew tired of his uncooperative ways, so they traded him. Less than two weeks after they had picked up Largent from Houston, the Seahawks sent Rashad to Minnesota for a 1977 fourth-round pick.

ROOKIE RECORDS

Two Seahawks quarterbacks have held the NFL record for passing yards by a rookie. Jim Zorn set a new mark in 1976 with 2,571 yards, and Rick Mirer had 2,833 in 1993. Mirer is now third on the list.

That pick became another wide receiver, Larry Seivers, but he also never played for the Seahawks, who traded him to Tampa Bay four months after they had drafted him. Then the Seahawks sent the 1979 fourth-round pick they had received from the Buccaneers to Buffalo as compensation for the Seahawks signing Rashad in 1976.

Thus, the Seahawks ended up with nothing for a guy who went on to make the Pro Bowl four times while catching at least 50 passes in each of his first six seasons. He went to his first Pro Bowl in 1978, the same year Largent first went to the all-star game for Seattle.

Rashad's best season was 1979, when his 80 receptions were second in the league and he was the most valuable player of the Pro Bowl. He was third in receiving yards (1,156) that season—the year the Seahawks could boast that Largent led the league (1,237).

While the Rashad deal did not turn out well, the Seahawks could always take solace in the fact that they had more than made up for it by getting a Hall of Fame receiver for almost nothing.

DEAL OR NO DEAL?

The Seahawks' most well-known trade that was never made was the deal that would have sent All-Pro safety Kenny Easley to the Phoenix Cardinals for Dave Krieg's successor. The Cardinals ended up sending Easley back when he failed a physical, and the rest is one of the saddest stories in Seahawks history. Easley had to retire with a kidney problem, and Kelly Stouffer turned into a waste of the three picks the Seahawks sent the Cardinals for him.

Stouffer was meant to be the "future" replacement for Krieg. But he wasn't the first guy the Seahawks tried to get to replace the undrafted quarterback from "now-defunct" Milton College. Even after Krieg had stepped in to lead the Seahawks to their first playoff berth in 1983, the team went after a guy from the Canadian Football League.

"I'd just played my worst game ever against the Raiders," Krieg said of Seattle's 30–14 loss to the Los Angeles Raiders in the AFC Championship Game. "I'm [home] in Wisconsin riding snowmobiles with a buddy a week later and find out they're going to bring in Warren Moon."

That's right, Warren Moon—the former Washington Husky who had just finished winning five Grey Cups with the Edmonton Eskimos. The strong-armed, 27-year-old quarterback who had thrown for 5,000 yards in each of the past two years and had 21,228 yards and 144 touchdowns in six seasons with Edmonton.

Moon quickly narrowed his choices to Seattle, where he had gone to college and still lived in the off-season, and Houston, where the Oilers had just hired Hugh Campbell—Moon's coach in Edmonton—to be their new coach.

Negotiations with the two teams dragged on for a month, and Krieg actually signed a new deal with the Seahawks in late January, before he even knew where Moon would land. Krieg had wanted to increase his salary to a level commensurate with what other starters in the league were making, and the Seahawks obliged him by bumping his annual pay from $85,000 to $250,000 in a new two-year contract.

Moon, meanwhile, was in line to get the richest deal in NFL history. And he ended up choosing the Oilers because they were willing to guarantee more of the contract. Both teams offered him $5.5 million over five years, the largest contract in NFL history at that time. But the Seahawks offered a signing bonus of just $1.1 million, while the Oilers guaranteed $4.5 million.

When Moon signed in early February, Krieg received a call from a friend telling him the news. Krieg's reply: "Good for

Warren. I'm so happy for him." Translation: "Yippee! I'm still the Seahawks' quarterback!"

The next time he saw Moon, Krieg told his fellow quarterback, "Thank you, Warren. I'm glad you went to Houston or I wouldn't be where I am today."

In 1984 Krieg put up better numbers than Moon, setting team records with 3,671 yards and 32 touchdowns and going to the first of three career Pro Bowls. He went on to become the Seahawks' career passing leader.

Of course, 13 years and eight Pro Bowls later, Moon did end up with the Seahawks. And then the Hall of Fame.

Wyman's Way Out

In 1987, the Seahawks had a glut of linebackers. Already on the squad were Pro Bowl linebacker Fredd Young and veterans Keith Butler, Bruce Scholtz, Greg Gaines, and Sam Merriman. Then they drafted Tony Woods in the first round and Dave Wyman in the second. And then they lucked into the first pick in the supplemental draft and chose Brian Bosworth.

Wyman thought he was all set to replace Butler at inside linebacker—until he heard about the Bosworth deal. He knew he had no chance of unseating the $11 million man or the Pro Bowl linebacker, who were starting together inside the Seahawks' 3-4 defense. So after the players returned from the strike in October, Wyman asked team president Mike McCormack for a trade.

McCormack accommodated his request and sent Wyman, a Stanford graduate, back to the Bay Area and to the San Francisco 49ers. Wyman's value actually had gone up since he was drafted earlier that year because teams knew a knee injury suffered in college was no longer a problem. So, a few months after using a second-round pick on him, the Seahawks were able to land second- and fourth-round picks from the 49ers.

But when he went down to San Francisco for his physical, an MRI on his shoulder indicated he needed surgery—another old college injury. The 49ers changed their offer to conditional second- and sixth-round picks, and McCormack said, "Forget it. Just send him back up here."

It turned out to be a good non-trade because the Seahawks were forced to deal Young before the 1988 season and Wyman stepped in as the starter and finished second on the team in tackles. He was a solid player, starting 43 games in five seasons with Seattle before finishing his career in Denver.

NOTES

The author would like to acknowledge the reporters who have covered the Seahawks over the years and whose reports were sometimes referenced for postgame quotes and details of games and other events. Special thanks to the work of Clare Farnsworth (*Post-Intelligencer*), Craig Smith and Jose Miguel Romero (*The Seattle Times*), and Mike Sando (*The News Tribune*). Also thanks to Greg Bishop of *The Seattle Times* for his assistance with contact information for interview subjects.

THE BLUE ANGEL

Safety Kenny Easley once said: "What separates Steve...": Smith, Don, "The Coffin Corner" (Professional Football Researchers Association, January 2007); www.footballresearch.com

"It took only seven months...": Smith, Don, "The Coffin Corner" (Professional Football Researchers Association, January 2007); www.footballresearch.com

STRIKE 3: PATERA'S OUT

"We have been disappointed...": *United Press International,* October 14, 1982.

"The strike gave us a chance...": *United Press International,* October 14, 1982.

NO OFFENSE, TEZ

The offense was so bad that...": "Seahawks Scrapbook Selections," *The Seattle Times*, December 31, 1992.

"It was like guys at Baskin-Robbins...": "Seahawks Scrapbook Selections," *The Seattle Times*, December 31, 1992.

FRANCHISE ON THE MOVE

"You sure would not take a team out of a place...": *The Associated Press*, August 31, 1988.

"I think Seattle is the greatest...": KING-TV as reported by *The Associated Press*, August 30, 1988.

"There is very serious concern on my part...": "League May Try to Stop Behring," *Seattle Post-Intelligencer*, February 10, 1996.

BLADES'S TRIALS

"It's something I will never put...": "For Blades, Shooting Will Always Be Backdrop...": *The Seattle Times*, July 22, 1996.

THE BOZ

"Seattle doesn't fit the mold...": *The Associated Press*, June 12, 1987.

"You very rarely get a chance...": "Boz Says He's Out to Get Elway," *The Denver Post*, September 8, 1987.

KRIEG'S DREAM DRIVE AND FREDDIE'S NIGHTMARE

"We could not tell whether...": "Zendejas Gets Another Chance," *Los Angeles Times*, January 4, 1988.

"I knew I had it.": *The Associated Press*, January 4, 1988.

"Our observation showed...": *The Associated Press*, January 4, 1988.

EASLEY'S END

"It was the right time...": "It Was the Right Time," *The Seattle Times*, October 16, 2002.

YOUNG WAS RESTLESS

"You're always concerned…": *The Associated Press*, September 9, 1988.

KRIEG AND SKANSI RUIN DERRICK'S DAY

"That last sack I didn't get…": *The Associated Press*, November 11, 1990.

"If he'd thrown it on time…": *The Associated Press*, November 11, 1990.

WIN AND THEY'RE IN

"If they don't go to church…": "A Win and a Prayer," *The Seattle Times*, December 28, 2003.

TWO GAMES, ONE LOSS

"We played like crap…": "A Shock to the System," *Seattle Post-Intelligencer*, October 11, 2004.

"You got a guy on the ropes…": "A Shock to the System," *Seattle Post-Intelligencer*, October 11, 2004.

ONE FOR THE BIRDS

"I thought we were making…": "In a Statement Game, Seahawks Left Speechless." *Seattle Post-Intelligencer*, November 24, 2003.

"That's how I was thinking.": "Ravens Given Extra Time," *Seattle Post-Intelligencer*, November 25, 2003.

WE WANT THE BALL, AND WE'RE GONNA SCORE!"

"To be honest with you, I'm dying inside…": "Packers Ice Seahawks on Interception Return," *Seattle Post-Intelligencer*, January 5, 2004.

A COMEBACK FUMBLED

"They have all been difficult…": "Seattle Reels in Loss," *The Denver Post*, December 20, 1999.

"Our playoffs have started.": "Mile-High Misery," *The Seattle Times*, December 20, 1999.

KICKED WHILE THEY WERE DOWN

"You could second-guess everything...": "Overtime and Out," *The* [Tacoma] *News Tribune,* January 15, 2007.

"It's a tough one...": "Overtime and Out," *The* [Tacoma] *News Tribune,* January 15, 2007.

THE BOGUS CALL THAT CHANGED IT ALL

"Because he had signaled a touchdown...": *The Associated Press,* December 7, 1998.

"Most definitely, he wasn't in.": *The Associated Press,* December 7, 1998.

SCORE ONE FOR THE REFS

"The play was ruled...": *The Associated Press,* September 17, 1990.

"Fernandez did not come down...": *The Associated Press,* September 17, 1990.

THE SUPER BOWL—XL CONTROVERSY

"We made our plays...": "Bitter End," *Seattle Post-Intelligencer,* February 6, 2006.

THE 12ᵀᴴ MAN

"Paul Brown voted for the rule...": "Seattle Coach Wants 'Dog Bone' Rule to Go with 'Noise' Rule," *United Press International,* September 6, 1989.

Jacob Green once said ...": "The Kingdome—Last hurrah," *The Seattle Times,* September 12, 1999.

"The fans were great to Seattle...": "Seahawks Finally Win, Bengals Finally Lose," *The Oregonian,* October 2, 1990.

"If you think last game was loud...": "The Sound by the Sound," *Seattle Post-Intelligencer,* September 21, 2006.

Quarterback Matt Hasselbeck said fans should...": "The Sound by the Sound," *Seattle Post-Intelligencer,* September 21, 2006.

"Loudest stadium I've ever been to...": *Hartford Courant,* September 24, 2006.

BUTTING HEADS WITH THE RAMS

"It's a throw-'em-up, scoring division...": "Offense New Focus," *Seattle Post-Intelligencer,* May 6, 2002.

"Coach Holmgren said, 'We'll win the game...'": "Alexander delivers on a special day," *The Seattle Times,* September 22, 2003.

"It feels like we just lost...": "A Shock to the System," *Seattle Post-Intelligencer,* October 11, 2004.

"This is a hard place for me to play.": *The Associated Press,* October 10, 2005.

THE PACKERS REUNION TOUR

"We obviously did it for our coach.": *The Associated Press,* November 2, 1999.

BATTLES WITH THE BENGALS

"Come on, Red.": "Bengals Beat Theatrical Seahawks," *Chicago Tribune,* January 1, 1989.

"Smart coaching by the Seahawks.": "Bengals Beat Theatrical Seahawks," *Chicago Tribune,* January 1, 1989.

MORE THAN TRUE VALUE

"Obviously a big piece to our puzzle...": "Finally, Mirer Is a Bear," *Seattle Post-Intelligencer,* February 19, 1997.

"We believe Rick has the qualities...": "Finally, Mirer Is a Bear," *Seattle Post-Intelligencer,* February 19, 1997.

"There has been only one other time...": "Cowboys Lasso Galloway," *The Columbus Dispatch,* February 13, 2000.

WHY'D THEY DO THAT?

"We think he'll be the quarterback of the future.": *The Associated Press,* April 23, 1988.

"They wanted Ahman. We needed a corner.": "Hawks Fill Secondary Need," *Seattle Post-Intelligencer,* April 15, 2000.

"I don't understand it at all.": "Dorsett Goes to Cowboys," *The Washington Post,* May 4, 1977.